ATD Soft Skills Series

Influence
in Talent Development

Vivian Blade

PRESS

Alexandria, VA

ATD Press is an internationally renowned source of insightful and practical information on talent development, training, and professional development.

ATD Press
1640 King Street
Alexandria, VA 22314 USA

Ordering information: Books published by ATD Press can be purchased by visiting ATD's website at td.org/books or by calling 800.628.2783 or 703.683.8100.

Library of Congress Control Number: 2021943871

ISBN-10: 1-952157-53-6
ISBN-13: 978-1-952157-53-0
e-ISBN: 978-1-952157-54-7

ATD Press Editorial Staff
Director: Sarah Halgas
Manager: Melissa Jones
Content Manager, Career Development: Lisa Spinelli
Developmental Editor: Kathryn Stafford and Jack Harlow
Production Editor: Hannah Sternberg
Text Design: Shirley E.M. Raybuck
Cover Design: John Anderson Jr.

Printed by BR Printers, San Jose, CA

Contents

About the Series

The world of work is changing. As companies once prioritized radical workplace performance and productivity improvements, they focused on training their employees with the purpose of getting more work done faster. But companies have learned that while their people might be increasingly productive, they aren't working better, particularly with each other. Lurking on the horizon is always greater automation, which will continue to shift the balance between the needs for hard and soft skills. Employees of the future will spend more time on activities that machines are less capable of, such as managing people, applying expertise, and communicating with others. More than ever, soft skills are being recognized as a premium.

Enter talent development.

TD professionals play a unique role in addressing the increasing demand for soft skills. They work with people and on behalf of people: A trainer facilitating a group of learners. A team of instructional designers working cross-functionally to address a business need. A learning manager using influence to make the case for increased budget or resources. But how can TD professionals expect to develop future employees in these soft skills if they're not developing their own?

At the Association for Talent Development (ATD), we're dedicated to creating a world that works better and empowering TD professionals like you to develop talent in the workplace. As part of this effort, ATD developed the Talent Development Capability Model, a framework to guide the TD profession in what practitioners need to know and do to develop themselves, others, and their organizations. While soft skills appear most prominently under the Building Personal Capability domain, these crucial skills cross every capability in the model, including those under Developing Professional Capability and Impacting Organizational Capability. Soft skills enable TD professionals to take their instructional design, training delivery and facilitation, future readiness, change management, and other TD capabilities to the next level.

Just as TD professionals need resources on how to develop talent, they need guidance in improving their interpersonal and intrapersonal skills—to be more adaptable, self-aware and empathetic, creative, team-oriented and collaborative, and influential and persuasive. This ATD series provides such guidance.

Organized with two parts, each book in the ATD Soft Skills Series tackles one soft skill that TD professionals need to foster in themselves to help the people and organizations they serve. Part 1 breaks down the skill into what it is, why it's important, and the internal or external barriers to improving it. Part 2 turns the lens on the daily work of TD professionals and how they can practice and perfect that skill on the job. Featuring worksheets, self-reflection exercises, and best practices, these books will empower TD professionals to build career resiliency by matching their technical expertise with newfound soft skill abilities.

Books in the series:
- *Adaptability in Talent Development*
- *Emotional Intelligence in Talent Development*
- *Creativity in Talent Development*
- *Teamwork in Talent Development*
- *Influence in Talent Development*

We're happy to bring you the ATD Soft Skills Series and hope these books support you in your future learning and development.

Jack Harlow, Series Editor
Senior Developmental Editor, ATD Press

Series Foreword

Oh, Those Misnamed Soft Skills!

For years organizations have ignored soft skills and emphasized technical skills, often underestimating the value of working as a team, communicating effectively, using problem solving skills, and managing conflict. New managers have failed because their promotions are often based on technical qualifications rather than the soft skills that foster relationships and encourage teamwork. Trainers as recently as a dozen years ago were reluctant to say that they facilitated soft skills training. Why?

Soft Skills: The Past and Now

The reluctance to admit to delivering (or requiring) soft skills often starts with the unfortunate name, "soft," which causes people to view them as less valuable than "hard" skills such as accounting or engineering. The name suggests they are easy to master or too squishy to prioritize developing. On both counts that's wrong. They aren't. In fact, Seth Godin calls them "real" skills, as in, "Real because they work, because they're at the heart of what we need today" (Godin 2017).

Yet, as a society, we seem to value technical skills over interpersonal skills. We tend to admire the scientists who discovered the vaccine for COVID-19 over leaders who used their communication skills to engage the workforce when they were quarantined at home. We easily admit to not knowing how to fly an airplane but readily believe we are creative or can adapt on the fly. We think that because we've been listening all our lives, we are proficient at it—when we're not. As a result, we put much more emphasis on developing our technical skills through advanced degrees and post–higher education training or certifications to land that first or next job than we do on mastering our interpersonal and intrapersonal skills.

Fortunately, many businesses and their leaders are now recognizing the value of having a workforce that has technical knowledge supported by soft skills. That's good because soft skills matter more to your career than you may envision. Consider: as a part of the Jobs Reset Summit, the World Economic Forum determined that 50 percent of the workforce needed reskilling and upskilling. The summit also identified the top 10 job reskilling needs for the future. Eight of the 10 required skills in the 21st century are nontechnical; these skills include creativity, originality, and initiative; leadership and social influence; and resilience, stress tolerance, and flexibility (Whiting 2020). LinkedIn's 2019 *Global Talent Trends Report* showed that acquiring soft skills is the most important trend fueling the future of the workplace: 91 percent of the respondents said that soft skills matter as much or more than technical skills and 80 percent believed they were critical to organizational success (Chandler 2019). A Deloitte report (2017) suggested that "soft skill–intensive occupations will account for two-thirds of all jobs by 2030" and that employees who practice skills associated with collaboration, teamwork, and innovation may be worth $2,000 more per year to businesses. As the cost of robots decreases and AI improves, soft skills like teamwork, problem solving, creativity, and influence will become more important.

Soft skills may not be as optional as one might originally imagine.

Soft Skills: Their Importance

Soft skills are sometimes referred to as enterprise skills or employability skills. Despite their bad rap, they are particularly valuable because they are transferable between jobs, careers, departments, and even industries, unlike hard or technical skills, which are usually relevant only to specific jobs. Communication often lands at the top of the soft skill list, but the category encompasses other skills, such as those included in the ATD Soft Skills Series: emotional intelligence, adaptability, teamwork, creativity, and influence. These personal attributes influence how well employees build trust, establish accountability, and demonstrate professional ethics.

Soft skills are also important because almost every job requires employees to interact with others. Organizations require a workforce that has technical skills and formal qualifications for each job; however, the truth is that business is about relationships. And, organizations depend on relationships to be successful. This is where successful employees, productive organizations, and soft skills collide.

Soft Skills and the Talent Development Capability Model

Talent development professionals are essential links to ensure that organizations have all the technical and soft skills that are required for success. I sometimes get exhausted just thinking about everything we need to know to ensure success for our organizations, customers, leaders, learners, and ourselves. The TD profession is no cookie-cutter job. Every day is different; every design is different; every delivery is different; and every participant is different. We are lucky to have these differences because these broad requirements challenge us to grow and develop.

As TD professionals, we've always known that soft skills are critical for the workforce we're responsible for training and developing. But what about yourself as a TD professional? What soft skills do you require to be effective and successful in your career? Have you ever thought about all the skills in which you need to be proficient?

ATD's Talent Development Capability Model helps you define what technical skills you need to improve, but you need to look beyond the short capability statements to understand the soft skills required to support each (you can find the complete model on page 29). Let's examine a few examples where soft skills are required in each of the domains.

- **Building Personal Capability** is dedicated to soft skills, although all soft skills may not be called out. It's clear that communication, emotional intelligence, decision making, collaboration, cultural awareness, ethical behavior, and lifelong learning are soft skills.

Project management may be more technical, but you can't have a successful project without great communication and teamwork.

- **Developing Professional Capability** requires soft skills throughout. Could instructional design, delivery, and facilitation exist without creativity? You can't coach or attend to career development without paying attention to emotional intelligence (EI) and influence. Even technology application and knowledge management require TD professionals to be adaptable, creative, and team players for success.

- **Impacting Organizational Capability** focuses on the soft skills you'll use while working at the leadership and organizational level. For you to have business insight, be a partner with management, and develop organizational culture, you will need to build teamwork with the C-suite, practice influencing, and use your EI skills to communicate with them. Working on a talent strategy will require adaptability and influence. And you can't have successful change without excellent communication, EI, and teamwork. Future readiness is going to require creativity and innovation.

Simply put, soft skills are the attributes that enable TD professionals to interact effectively with others to achieve the 23 capabilities that span the spectrum of disciplines in the Capability Model.

Soft Skills: The Key to Professionalism

So, as TD professionals we need to be proficient in almost all soft skills to fulfill the most basic responsibilities of the job. However, there's something even more foundational to the importance of developing our soft skills: Only once we've mastered these skills can we project the professionalism that will garner respect from our stakeholders, our learners, and our peers. We must be *professional*, or why else are we called *TD professionals?*

Professionalism is the driving force to advance our careers. To earn the title of TD professional we need to be high performers and exhibit the qualities and skills that go beyond the list of technical TD skills. We need to be soft-skill proficient to deliver services with aplomb. We need to be team members to demonstrate we work well with others. We need to be EI-fluent to ensure that we are aware of, control, and express our emotions and handle interpersonal relationships well. We need to be creative to help our organization achieve a competitive advantage. We need to be adaptable to future-proof our organizations. And we need influencing skills that help us earn that proverbial seat at the table.

We all need role-specific knowledge and skills to perform our jobs, but those who achieve the most are also proficient in soft skills. You will use these skills every day of your life, in just about every interaction you have with others. Soft skills allow you to demonstrate flexibility, resourcefulness, and resilience—and as a result, enhance your professionalism and ensure career success. And a lack of them may just limit your career potential.

Clearly, soft skills are more critical than once thought and for TD professionals and trainers they are likely to be even more critical. Your participants and customers expect you to be on the leading edge of most topics that you deliver. And they also expect you to model the skills required for a successful career. So, which soft skills do you need to become a *professional* TD professional? Is it clearer communication? Interpersonal savvy? Increased flexibility? Self-management? Professional presence? Resourcefulness?

E.E. Cummings said, "It takes courage to grow up and become who you really are." I hope that you have the courage to determine which skills you need to improve to be the best trainer you can be—and especially to identify those misnamed soft skills that aren't *soft* at all. Then establish standards for yourself that are high enough to keep you on your training toes. The five books in the ATD Soft Skills Series offer you a great place to start.

Elaine Biech, Author
Skills for Career Success: Maximizing Your Potential at Work

Introduction

Tanisha, a talent development leader, had been with her company for six years and had nearly a decade of industry experience. She had worked in talent development her entire career and was very passionate about her profession. She had come to know a lot of people across the organization from her interactions through her role, and loved her job because of the variety of projects and departments her work touched.

With her knowledge of the company and industry and prior work experience, she thought her credentials would give her a pretty easy road, expecting that people would be quickly receptive to her observations, ideas, and recommendations. It often didn't work out that way. She didn't yet realize how much influence would play a part in her ability to be successful. Her deficient skill at influence left her frustrated and sometimes feeling like she had to work harder to get things done. Influence was critical in moving leaders to accept her team's talent development recommendations. Influence was also critical to inspiring participants in her programs to adopt the ideas and strategies shared.

Tanisha knew she had to get better at influencing. She did some research on how to influence and paid particular attention when observing other people's styles. She discovered myriad approaches, from the coercive, such as intimidating, insisting, or forcing compliance, to the cooperative, such as collaborating or negotiating. In her day-to-day work, Tanisha looked for various opportunities to try different influence approaches. Some worked better than others, and the more coercive tactics left her feeling uneasy. She learned from her mistakes and successes and was determined to become a respected person of influence. But she wouldn't stop there. She was committed to sharing what she learned with others.

Tanisha discovered that treating influence as simply a tactic might not result in the outcomes she wanted. There was more to influence than meets the eye. It's those lessons learned and Tanisha's journey to becoming a respected person of influence that we are going to explore in this book. What has been your experience with influence? What lessons learned have inspired your approach?

What Have I Learned About Influence?

In my years of experience as a leader and talent development professional, I've come to realize the importance of the skill of influence. My journey has been a lot like Tanisha's: observing, seeking advice from mentors, and learning by trial and error. In the junior years of my career, I was learning to influence among my peers and spent a lot of time trying to influence at levels senior to my position. As I advanced, I learned that influence doesn't automatically come with a title. Honoring and respecting others and being focused on making a meaningful contribution earned the greatest influence.

Three roles in my career stand out as the greatest influence learning opportunities. Two of those roles were when I worked for General Electric.

When I was mid-career, I stepped into a role as product manager for sourced cooking products. My job involved P&L responsibility for many of the niche products within the cooking portfolio. In addition to using our own manufacturing facilities, we partnered with other manufacturers around the world to produce specialty cooktops, range hoods, and compact ranges. As a product manager, I worked with a team across all levels and functions of the company, such as engineering, industrial design, manufacturing, quality, service, finance, marketing, and sales, none of whom reported directly to me. I worked with manufacturers in Asia, Mexico, Canada, and Europe. I also had to compete for funding and other resources. With primary responsibility for all aspects of this product portfolio, influence became critical to developing and executing our product strategy successfully. I had to build trust and engage people in a way that showed how much I valued not only their ideas and contributions, but also each person as a human being.

The second role I had within GE taught me even more about influence. As head of the customer experience initiative for the consumer and industrial division, I worked with a team across all business units and functions. Sometimes the feedback from customers was difficult to hear and there would be pushback. In some cases, improving the customer experience required considering investments that weren't planned or budgeted. Rather than insisting or persuading that certain action be taken, my team did a lot of listening, facilitated many discussions and ideation sessions, and worked hard to build partnerships.

After my career with GE, I launched a talent development and coaching practice and have had the privilege of working with clients to ensure they have the human capital and supporting systems to remain relevant, competitive, and growing. I work with leaders to develop policies and programs, to design and deliver training and coaching based on an assessment of needs, and to grow organizational capacity for ongoing success. Through this work, I realized that talent development has an important role to play in influencing the economic viability of organizations and global economies.

I have learned firsthand how influence derives from our connections with others. We may not speak directly to someone, or our interactions with others may be short. In what seems like inconsequential times, we are still influencing. Influence comes not simply from fulfilling the responsibilities of our jobs. Talent development professionals have the opportunity to influence at a deeper level. You have the potential to influence the behaviors of individuals in a way that can shift organizational culture.

Influencing Change

Successful change requires influencing others' perspectives, buy-in, and behaviors. Through your training programs, you instruct people in how to be more productive, how to hone their technical skills, and how to skillfully manage projects and improve their operating results. Even as more technology is introduced to make organizations run more efficiently, work cannot get done without the people involved in the processes. Organizations are recognizing that their most important assets are their employees, customers, and partners. The experiences they have, largely affected by personal interactions and relationships, significantly impact operating outcomes such as commitment, retention, productivity, service levels, and revenue. People want to feel valued, included, appreciated, and purposeful. Creating an environment where that can take place requires skills such as emotional intelligence, trust, teamwork, adaptability, and influence. Talent development professionals have the opportunity to be role models and to develop these skills in others.

Influence ≠ Positional Power

Especially when not in an official position of power, you may not view yourself as a strong influencer, and, therefore, lack the confidence that you can be the conduit to change. However, the influence that can be generated without positional power has the greatest potential for impact. You're called upon in sometimes subtle ways every day to influence the people and the environment around you. The compound effect of small instances of influence can make the greatest impact in your workplace, your community, and your home.

As you often find yourself in situations where you can influence others, be careful about how you use that influence. Influence can be used to exert power over others or can most effectively be used to engage others. Whether it's consulting with senior leaders, developing rising leaders, or coaching a professional to rediscover their purpose, how you inclusively engage with and inspire the best in others is your greatest opportunity and reward. You influence the thinking, behaviors, and actions of people, whether intentionally or unintentionally.

The current environment of our organizations is changing rapidly. COVID-19 forever changed the way we work and learn. The digital transformation has connected us in ways unimaginable just a few years before the pandemic, accelerating the speed of the transition to greater numbers of employees working remotely. The virtual classroom and online learning have become commonplace. Skills gaps for a more global and tech-driven economy are requiring employers to retool and upskill their workforce. Calls for social justice are reshaping organizational culture to be more inclusive and equitable. The role of talent development professionals in their ability to influence in this environment has never been more important and palpable. You have a front row seat, leading the work that allows organizations and professionals to successfully operate in this uncertain, ever-evolving reality.

How This Book Can Help You

My focus on the skill of influence deepened when it began to surface in conversations and in my research about skill set gaps. I was working with a client on the design of a leadership development program. As we reviewed their needs assessment, influence appeared as an essential skill that was underdeveloped within the organization. As we were planning for a relaunch after COVID-19 had halted another client's leadership development program, feedback from participants revealed influence had become an elevated challenge for them in the adapted environment. Reviewing various research reports on women in the workplace illuminated influence as an opportunity for further development.

My content development process included exploring my personal experience, observations, secondary research, and conversations with others about their experiences. In preparation for this book, I interviewed seasoned leaders who had experience with influence in the talent development profession. From this work, I discovered a handful of principles and associated practices that can enhance and broaden a person's influence. These are the principles I reveal to you in the pages that follow.

As you discover and begin to adopt these principles, you will be better positioned to elevate your influence in your work and personal life. You'll find that you can be more effective at getting things done through others. You don't have to use or be in a position of authority in order to move people. You have the ability within you to have influence. By implementing the principles in this book, your influence can build among your peers, among those who lead, and among team members you lead.

How to Use This Book

In this book, my goal is to inspire you in growing your personal influence and provide a framework to develop the skill of influence within your organizations. I want you to become that person of influence who has a greater positive impact on people's lives and the organizations you work with and lead.

In part 1, chapters 1–3, we examine how influence is a critical skill. We begin in chapter 1 exploring what it means to influence, the essence of building a foundation of trust and personal connection in a professional environment. Chapter 2 investigates why influence matters in the workplace and explores the science behind how influence works and the approaches used. We also consider the ethics of influence. Chapter 3 unpacks the barriers to influence. I'll point out the three mistakes sabotaging your influence, and show you what to watch out for to avoid stepping into these traps.

Part 2, chapters 4–9, reveals the five Influence With SCALE Principles and the role influence plays in talent development. In chapter 4, I introduce the framework of the five powerful influence principles and their role in becoming a person of influence. I pull back the curtain on the details of each of the principles in chapters 5 through 9 with specific actions to scale your influence for greater impact:

- **S: social capital.** Dividends from the consistent investments you make in growing mutual, selfless relationships built on a foundation of empathy, genuine concern, respect, and trust.

- **C: courage.** Facing uncertainty, you are willing to take that step forward, even though the road ahead is full of more questions than answers.
- **A: authenticity.** Guided by your values and principles, you are more self-aware and astutely conscientious and consistent in your interactions with others.
- **L: leaning in with passion.** You are invested in a meaningful purpose that inspires you to give your best effort.
- **E: engaging a diverse and inclusive workplace community.** You invite, welcome, and engage peoples' uniqueness to inspire an inclusive workplace community.

In chapter 10, I share steps for how to personalize your action plan toward becoming a recognized person of influence and growing influence skills across your organization. In the resources section of the appendix, you'll have the opportunity to rate your current practice in the influence principles and can access several job aids, tools, and resources to help you begin taking steps toward an accelerated transformation. (Resources are also downloadable at InfluenceWithScale.com.)

Whether you're early in your career or a seasoned professional, your ability to influence will dictate your success in your role and in your career progression.

PART 1
The Meaning of Influence

CHAPTER 1

What It Means to Influence

Consuela, director of customer service, was facing an increasing workload and two vacant positions. Her team was stretched thin and working extra hours, leaving her no choice but to push out their deadlines. It was true that the company was growing, adding new products and serving new industries. But the expansion had introduced challenges with product quality, logistics, and customer education, which only increased the volume of work for her team. Consuela was concerned about their ability to get everything done while maintaining quality, but she was especially worried about the potential for increased stress.

To help her team, first Consuela tried the obvious things, like shuffling a couple of projects among different team members with lighter workloads. But it wasn't enough. Other departments were creating these issues for customers, and Consuela needed to persuade their managers to act. Her team simply couldn't satisfy all the customer requests they were receiving. While she knew her people lacked information and training, she hoped they could stay focused and committed, to hang in there even on the most chaotic days.

At her wit's end, Consuela knew she didn't have the power to solve this problem. She decided to reach out to Tanisha, her colleague and frequent confidante in the talent development department, for advice.

Tanisha could see that, to relieve the pressure on her team quickly, Consuela favored short-term solutions. However, this wasn't necessarily a short-term solution type of problem. Tanisha had to convince Consuela that this was going to take some time, especially in getting other department leaders to work with her. Many would see this as Consuela's staffing problem rather than an organizational problem. Consuela had to help them see otherwise.

How can influence play a role in resolving Consuela's dilemma?

Influence in Practice

What is influence? *Merriam Webster's Dictionary* defines it as "the act or power of producing an effect without apparent exertion of force or direct exercise of command." When you influence, you are effectively offering your ideas and perspectives so that you move someone to a mutually beneficial outcome in their actions, behavior, opinions, or beliefs. Though the intent in influencing is to move people, there is power in influence. Use that power carefully and responsibly. Don't be misled into thinking that you, as one individual, can't make much of a difference to others. You can. And, you do. The question is, what type of person of influence will you be?

Jimmy Nelson, corporate director of organizational development and training with a multinational company, defines influence as "the ability to motivate or move somebody in a positive direction that you see as an advantage for them and you. You have to build that foundation of a good relationship where there's trust and understanding that you're there to help them and don't want anything in return."

Being a person of influence is more about how you live, adding value to those around you, rather than simply what you do to advance an agenda. Influence takes time. Influence is not always an active, intentional endeavor. Your influence is deeply affected by what people observe in you. Depending on your goal, intentional attempts to influence someone may involve a tactic, such as persuading or negotiating. A tactic is a tool, method, or approach that you employ in attempts to achieve a desired outcome. Those tactics will be more effective when people have a history with each other, and your intentions are deemed honorable. Therefore, influence as a process goes beyond the tactics used.

Influence: Persistently in Demand

Have you ever felt like you've walked in Consuela's or Tanisha's shoes? Even on a smaller scale, the need for influence shows up daily. You are the target of influence throughout each day. And you are regularly attempting to influence others.

Let's consider a day in your life. As you attempt to wake up in the morning, your schedule for the day influences your decision to sleep in for just a few more minutes. If you have children, you try to convince them that it's time to wake up. You turn on the radio or television to the news. The news reports influence your perceptions of your community and even the world. The advertisements come on and attempt to influence your buying decisions. The commercial for that fancy new sports car or the vehicle that better accommodates your growing family tempts you to visit the dealer. The commercials for a popular restaurant entice you to stop by to pick up breakfast on your way to work.

You also make your routine stop at Starbucks. While waiting in line, a woman next to you is savoring her cup of coffee. You ask, "What are you having?" "A creamy caffe latte," she says. "Delicious," you reply. That's what you order. When you get to work, a co-worker alerts you that you're needed in a meeting that wasn't originally on your calendar for the day. You're briefed on the issues and decide you need to be there. You attend a virtual lunch meeting where the speaker presents some new ideas and strategies. You consider how the strategies could be useful for your team.

Next on your calendar are information-gathering interviews to address a concern with an internal client. You ask the data analyst on your team to help gather data on another project and determine conclusions from the insights. You plan to join colleagues for dinner after work. After weighing several suggestions, one colleague highly recommends a particular restaurant given his experience. That's where you meet.

When you arrive home after dinner, your 10-year-old daughter is still at the dinner table, refusing to eat her vegetables. There are dishes in the sink that need to be washed, but your teenager is deep into his homework and says he doesn't have time to do them. The dog is waiting by the door to go for your walk. Alas, bedtime. You want to catch the end of the movie you were watching over the weekend. As you navigate to make the selection, a short clip of another movie grabs your attention. You watch that one instead.

You don't even think about it. You go about your day being influenced and have myriad opportunities to influence. All these occurrences influence your thinking, decisions, and actions—some to your liking, and some maybe to your regret.

In fact, in his book, *To Sell Is Human: The Surprising Truth About Moving Others* (2012), Daniel H. Pink shared the following results from his survey, "What Do You Do at Work?": "People are now spending about 40 percent of their time at work engaged in nonsales selling—persuading, influencing, and convincing others in ways that don't involve a direct purchase," and they "consider this aspect of their work crucial to their professional success."

Therefore, influence is a skill you want to become good at.

Our Personal Experience With Influence

As you think back over the course of your life, recall what most influenced who you are today. What kind of impression did these familiar sources of influence have on your life?

Close to Home

These are the people who have been most influential on your development as you grew, such as your parents, of course, but likely others. They include mentors and sponsors as you've grown in your education and career. Your most favorable memories are of those who were role models, influencing you most notably by their character and values.

I recall the teacher who encouraged me and some of the other girls in my class to take advanced math classes and accounting in high school.

From that experience, I was well prepared for college-level math when I arrived at Berea College and decided to major in business. That has led to a successful career in business.

Larger Than Life

Prominent figures in our history and present-day culture often have an influence within our lives. (Think Abraham Lincoln, Mahatma Gandhi, Marie Curie, Dr. Martin Luther King Jr., and Nelson Mandela.) The life work of such individuals has led to seismic shifts in society. In many cases, they are cultural icons.

Their courage reminds us of what is possible and often inspires us to champion or support causes that are important to us, whether on a national stage or within our own communities. Volunteering with non-profit organizations is an ideal way to give back and make a broader impact outside of your immediate circle.

The Invisible Made Visible

Lastly, beyond people, we are heavily influenced by culture, practices, laws, regulations, policies, and even our biases and stereotypes. Beliefs influence how each of these factors are shaped. And it's a two-way street; these factors influence our beliefs, behaviors, and actions. As you grow up in a culture, you are taught certain beliefs and norms that you are expected to follow. As you join different organizations across your career, you'll find that each has its own unique culture, policies, and practices that you are expected to align with.

Among the core values of one of the organizations I work with is "have fun." While they are focused on being a high-performing organization, it's also important to create a work environment employees enjoy. What people do at work and how they interact are heavily influenced by this value.

Much like the influences on you across your life, your influence can shift the perspectives or behaviors of others. You may not realize the impact you're having on another person. Know that others are watching you and take cues from your words and behavior.

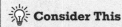

Consider This

As you think about your life, who were the people and what were the experiences that most influenced who you are today?

Are You an Influencer or a Person of Influence?

With all the personal experiences you've had with influence, you likely have some firsthand perspectives on how you might answer this question. An influencer is often described as someone with a goal or outcome in mind who is good at moving others to their way of thinking or to take a certain action. Influencers may not always be people. Various brands attempt to get consumers to buy their products and services, many using social media influencers to do so. This relatively new phenomenon has grown into a multibillion-dollar industry and continues to expand as social media becomes more and more entrenched in people's lives. "As e-commerce and social media converge, influencers will become increasingly vital intermediaries, helping to connect brands with consumers on social media in highly resonant, authentic ways that can deliver immediate returns," according to *Business Insider* (2021). Social media influencers shape your behavior and buying decisions based on their recommendations and the lifestyles they appear to have by using the brands they represent. Because they often hold celebrity status, there is a greater tendency to trust their judgment and associate their expertise with the recommendation. Also, we may aspire to associate ourselves with products that make us appear popular or successful.

There are times when all of us are influencers. You need to move people within a short timeframe. You may have a decision that needs to be made or an action that needs to be taken. You attempt to exercise an approach that will most likely accomplish your objective. For example, you might use data from employee feedback that supports a recommendation for a new performance management process. Then, you might have individuals who have a closer relationship with the decision makers speak in support of your recommendations. Those are viable, common approaches.

Alternatively, when describing a person of influence, we see someone we look up to, in many cases because of personal interest. These individuals were often role models, someone we could learn from. They may have been a mentor, a manager who genuinely cared about our success, or a visible figure within our company who was respected and looked out for the best interest of all employees. Even if you don't know the person of influence well personally, they have proven that they are trustworthy as you observe them over time.

If you are recognized as a person of influence, that foundation of trust we discussed earlier may put you in a position to depend less on influence tactics because your opinion is highly regarded. In the example of recommending a new performance management process, the decision makers may have had some experience in working with you in the past. You have consistently demonstrated that you are knowledgeable and have the best intentions of the organization in mind. You have a reputation that aligns with the organization's values and priorities. You may need to depend less on others to establish your credibility. The degree to which you are effective at moving others is enhanced by investing time and energy toward adding value.

In his article "Being an Influencer and Being Influential Are Not the Same Thing" (2019), Robert K. Baggs says that "Success as either an influencer or influential figure can look strikingly similar on the face of things, but scratch below the surface and where one hollows out, the other goes deeper." The influential person wants to make a difference and will teach others what they know and are passionate about. If you want to have a successful career, according to Baggs, "aim not for the coveted influencer title, but rather emanating influence as a direct result of your worth and value being recognized and appreciated by your community, be that locally or in a global field."

Summary

Who you have become is a product of the influences on you from various aspects in your life—from the people around you to the environment you grew up in and currently live and work in. Similarly, whether intentional or not, you have an influence on other people. A key question for you to consider is, are you an influencer or a person of influence? Influence goes beyond the tactic you may choose to move someone toward a certain belief or to take a desired action. Greater influence is achieved as you are regarded as a person of influence, earning a foundation of trust from adding value to those around you. Read on to understand why this distinction is so important to your success.

CHAPTER 2

Why Influence Matters

On the advice of Tanisha, her colleague in talent development, customer service manager Consuela decided to meet with Daniel, the head of supply chain. Consuela shared data on the increased volume of calls, emails, and chat messaging requests about product availability, delivery, and quality that had inundated her team. But Daniel was skeptical. To him, Consuela was shifting blame for something that was her responsibility. He suggested she try to take greater care of her own staff and improve their processes. Daniel thought the volume increase was a result of a normal sales increase and routine new-customer questions. Their discussion got a little defensive and tense at times, and they left the meeting with nothing resolved and no agreement to meet again.

Consuela's frustrations were growing. How could Daniel not see that this was a problem? What else could she do to convince him that something had to be done? Her team couldn't continue to work at these volumes. She didn't have enough budget to hire extra staff. And, besides, that wouldn't fix the problems anyway. Customers were going to lose their patience if this continued much longer.

When Consuela told Tanisha about Daniel's reaction, Tanisha realized she had some work to do. To determine the right approach, she would need to observe Consuela and the customer service team as well as figure out how to use the strong working relationship with Daniel she had built over the years. The worst thing that could happen now would be for Consuela to alienate allies when she needed them most.

Influence: An Essential Soft Skill

As work is being done more and more in teams and projects, organizations are becoming flatter, and influence increasingly has become a critical skill to function in this type of environment. Your ability to move people toward a common objective, whether or not they are within your direct authority, is essential to getting things done. In her book *The Art of Quiet Influence* (2019), Jocelyn Davis describes influence as "the ability to engage and guide others in collaborative work without relying on personal authority." Influence can be most effective when approached in this way.

The workplace benefits of influence as a soft skill are many yet subtle. Just for starters, ask yourself: Could influence help your team be more effective together? Could influence help you be heard in a meeting? And if you're a manager, could influence make you more appreciated? The answer to all these questions is yes.

You probably know that if someone reports to you, they don't want to be micromanaged, always being told what to do, when to do it, and how to do it. People may comply with what they are being asked to do, though they may not agree with it. But you won't get the best of what is possible for them to contribute unless you engage their head and their heart. So how do you do it? When you can connect with someone at a deeper level, you tap into what they care about and believe in. You seek a shared connection and demonstrate that you value them.

As a talent development professional, your work may often involve the need to influence other professionals across all levels of an organization without the direct authority to drive compliance. "Gratefully, I realized early on in my career that as a learning leader, the only way I can impact business results is through influence because I don't make money for the company," explains Sandi Maxey, vice president, and director of talent development, Sandy Spring Bank. "I don't produce anything of salable value, so the only way I can be impactful is by my influence. We don't make the music. We just guide people to make the music." Sandi's statement is a powerful reminder for talent development professionals. Your direct impact on the bottom line is often heavily dependent on how you influence others.

The Science of Influence and Persuasion

For decades, social scientists have been studying how we interact and use influence and persuasion in the many social arenas of our lives. Leadership expert Claudio Feser discusses nine tactics of influence in his book *When Execution Isn't Enough: Decoding Inspirational Leadership* (2016).

Three of these tactics Feser refers to as hard tactics, which are more focused on the influencer:

- **Requesting.** Influencing others by using positional power to confidently and assertively direct the actions of others. Reflective of what Feser refers to as "command and control" leadership, requesting requires reminding people and following up to ensure compliance.
- **Legitimating.** Influencing others by establishing authority or credibility based on compliance with official company policies or procedures.
- **Coalition.** Influencing others by building support among a network of people and citing the names of those supporters to impress upon those you wish to influence. Letting them know that others have gone along with your request or idea, and they should also.

The next six tactics Feser calls the soft tactics. As you work through them, they grow from being focused on the influencer's motivations to being more focused on the perspectives and motivations of the persons being influenced:

- **Rational persuasion.** Influencing others by using data, facts, and rationale to justify a position and to show that one's perspective makes the most sense.

- **Socializing.** Influencing others by warmly showing an interest in them, being friendly, and building rapport and relationships. Attempting to be more likable.
- **Personal appeal.** Influencing others by requesting support based on the loyalty and trust of their friendship or relationship.
- **Exchanging.** Influencing others by appealing to something that is important to them in return for a favor. Based on the concept of reciprocity, you may compromise to create a win-win situation.
- **Consultation.** Influencing others by getting them engaged in providing suggestions, and acting on those suggestions, to develop the course of action. Consultation is a form of participative leadership.
- **Inspirational appeal.** Influencing others by appealing to their values, ideals, and emotions. Inspirational appeal is a form of inspirational leadership.

Feser found that rational persuasion is the most commonly used influence approach. He says the hard leadership approaches—requesting, coalition, and legitimating—create high levels of compliance yet little or no true commitment to action and change. In times of ambiguity, complexity, and rapid change, Feser suggests that inspirational leadership, which builds on inspirational appeals, may be needed most.

Social scientist and expert in influence and persuasion Robert Cialdini introduced the six principles of persuasion in his seminal book, *Influence: The Psychology of Persuasion* (1984). Through his primary research studying what he refers to as compliance professionals (such as sales operators, fundraisers, recruiters, and advertisers), he found that among the vast array of approaches people use to influence others, they all fall into six basic categories, which he refers to as the six principles of persuasion:

- **Liking.** If people like you—because they sense you like them or because of things you have in common—they're more apt to say yes to you.

- **Reciprocity.** People tend to return favors. If you help people, they'll help you. If you behave in a certain way (cooperatively, for example), they'll respond in kind.
- **Social proof.** People will do things they see other people doing—especially if those people seem similar to them.
- **Commitment and consistency.** People want to be consistent, or at least to appear to be. If they make a public voluntary commitment, they'll try to follow through.
- **Authority.** People defer to experts and to those in positions of authority (and typically underestimate their tendency to do so).
- **Scarcity.** People value things more if they perceive them to be scarce.

"Each category is governed by a fundamental psychological principle that directs human behavior and, in doing so, gives the tactics their power," Cialdini explains. Therefore, he found, there is universal applicability of these six approaches across cultures and situations. These approaches, as well as identifying the opportune moments to engage them, can be learned. In his book *Pre-Suasion: A Revolutionary Way to Influence and Persuade* (2016), Cialdini shares additional research on how variables such as attention and association help to create the conditions for "privileged moments," which he describes as "points in time when an individual is particularly receptive to a communicator's message." For example, in simple interactions such as when you seek advice from your manager or ask a favor of a colleague, understanding the elements of "pre-suasion" in those circumstances could help you have a more successful interaction.

We see from these studies that there are various approaches you can use in your attempts to influence other people. Factors such as the context of the situation, people involved, relationship with the individuals, and objective will be among the considerations in your selections.

Social psychologist Andrew Luttrell offers some insight from current brain research that helps explain why we also favor one message over another, and why we might be more receptive to Cialdini's message. Studies find that our brain's ventromedial prefrontal cortex (vMPFC) is engaged when we are thinking about ourselves and is important to persuasion. "We've known for a long time that when communicators tailor their messages to the unique values of their audience, they can have more influence. And new evidence suggests that this is because these tailored messages activate the same self-focused brain areas that we know enhance persuasion" (Luttrell 2020).

So the approach you use in influencing matters. Values are an inherent part of the influence process, which takes us to the topic of ethics. The relationship that exists between people and the extent to which parties are concerned that the relationship is maintained impact the influence approach used.

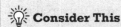 **Consider This**
- What influence approaches do you tend to use?
- Is there an approach that has worked more favorably than others? Why do you think this is so?

The Ethics of Influence

I watched a leader for a major consumer goods company interact with employees as she went through the office. She knew the names of many of the employees and stopped to check in on family or ask about someone's recent vacation. People gravitated to her because she had invested in building genuine connections with them. She had built a tremendous amount of trust from demonstrating that, even in the toughest of situations, she was selfless in her motives. In other words, she was an ethical influencer.

What are ethics? And how do they relate to influence? Luttrell (2020) says:

Ethics represents the moral code that guides a person's choices and behaviors throughout their life. The idea of a moral code extends beyond the individual to include what is determined to be right, and wrong, for a community or society at large. Ethics is concerned with rights, responsibilities, use of language, what it means to live an ethical life, and how people make moral decisions.

Heavily developed from your core values and the environment around you, your personal ethics act as a GPS that influences your thoughts, perspectives, decisions, words, behaviors, and actions, both unconsciously and consciously. Your moral code of ethics becomes foundational to who you are and what you represent. It plays out in your day-to-day interactions with others and influences your reputation.

Ethics are extremely important to building influence. You must consider not only what is ethical in your eyes but also what is ethical in the eyes of the individuals you are engaging, and the culture and environment in which you are operating. For example, your personal ethics might include integrity, loyalty, equality, fairness, empathy, and respect. Each of these represents a quality that would be critical to ethical influence.

Cialdini (1984) cautions against exploiting his persuasive approaches and emphasizes the opportunity to strengthen relationships and have greater influence when applying them ethically. He also warns that with the "ever-accelerating pace and informational crush of modern life," people will be more willing to be influenced before carefully thinking about what they are complying to, a form of what he calls "mindless compliance." Therefore, each of us has a responsibility in how we use influence, not to take advantage of those we influence, but to inform and invite.

Your motivation for influencing is a direct representation of your ethics. Is your intended outcome to help or to harm? Is it only for personal gain or will the lives of others be better as a result?

What's Your Approach to Influence?

The degree to which people are more informed is shaping how the influence process is evolving. Influence is not a one-sided proposition. It should be an exchange of ideas and perspectives that are reflected on and validated, around which decisions have been made. Prior to the digital transformation, information was primarily held by the person doing the influencing. For example, when you went to buy a camera, the salesperson had most of the information about the brands and product selections they sold in the store. You gained increased knowledge of available options as you visited different retailers. In today's environment, information is readily available and the selection of retailers to purchase from is more expansive. The buyer holds greater power to negotiate in the process. The time of influence through limited information is ending.

You may use a variety of approaches to influence given a situation. In your role as a talent development professional, what you are aiming for is a deeper, lasting influence. Your goal is to inspire commitment, not mislead or coerce into compliance. Influence requires an investment in your intention to build a reputation worthy of trust.

Summary

To be successful in the evolving workplace, influence plays an essential role. A number of tactics are often used in attempts to influence others, the most common of which are persuasive in nature. Because of the potential impact of your influence, you must consider the ethics associated with your approach. As a person of influence, your intention is to seize the influence opportunity to strengthen relationships and achieve mutually beneficial outcomes. This intention becomes your north star, helping you avoid the barriers to influence discussed in chapter 3.

CHAPTER 3

Barriers to Influence

Morale was at an all-time low on Consuela's customer service team. The team members continued to be frustrated by their workload and customer interactions. And now Consuela worried that they no longer saw her as their ally. Several of her team had been with the company for years and had built relationships with many customers. While Consuela valued her employees' experience and passion for customer service, she was having difficulty convincing any other leaders of her operational concerns, let alone customer service staffing issues.

Consuela became relentless, sending daily reports of customer service volumes and issues to Daniel, the supply chain manager. She finally got Daniel to assign an intern to work with her. Not what she had hoped, but at least she finally had more staff. Once they got some of the analysis done, though, Daniel's intern had no authority or resources to go any further. It was back to the drawing board.

When Consuela met with Tanisha, the L&D head quickly picked up on some mistakes Consuela was making. These were errors that Tanisha had experienced firsthand.

Three Mistakes Sabotaging Your Influence

As is the case with Consuela, three common mistakes often surface with my coaching clients when they're trying to influence others to their point of view or agenda. What they soon realize is that these mistaken mindsets and approaches sabotage their influence rather than enhance it:

1. **Mistake manipulation for influence.** These people believe they must manipulate others to persuade them to their position. They see influence as a win/lose deal. This is the fastest way to turn others against you. People can tell when they're being sold.
2. **Believe influence is instant.** Others believe influence is like making instant coffee. Just add water and stir. They think all it takes is standing in front of people and making their case or twisting arms. Any influence that results is surface level and suspect.
3. **Treat influence as a transaction.** Some people treat influence as if they're closing a deal . . . once their subject is sold, their work is done.

Do you find yourself falling into these traps? How have they turned out for you?

Let's explore these mistakes further.

Mistake Manipulation for Influence

One day early on after starting my talent development practice, I answered a call from a person who touted himself as a marketing expert. He caught me at just the right time, as I was in need of advice for how to best market my business. He asked me about the challenges and frustrations in my current approach to marketing and told me how his strategies would solve all my problems. He walked me through how to get started in his program and told me I had to make a decision "today" to get his best offer. I took the bait, gave him my credit card number and closed the deal. As we started working together, our first couple of calls went fine. Then, he became unresponsive and was hard to reach. He didn't follow through on what he promised he'd do for me. I'd been manipulated. I felt angry, stupid, and embarrassed. Getting my money back took going through the Better Business Bureau. Though the total dollars involved weren't significant, being hoodwinked left a bad taste in my mouth. If this is what I had to do to influence others in my business, I didn't like it. It wasn't congruent with my values or who I am.

Think back to those times when someone has tried to influence or persuade you. Which experiences most stand out? Likely the ones that left you feeling manipulated. What often comes to mind are memories of having encountered a pushy used-car salesman or those repeated annoying telemarketing calls. Even more vivid are the negative political ads during election season that seem to permeate every commercial break when you're watching your favorite show or YouTube channel. Politicians use what seems like every negative tactic against their opponent to win your vote. And, of course, there are times at work when someone tries to manipulate you to go along with their position.

In most, if not all, of these situations, you felt like you were being coerced into making a decision that you weren't necessarily ready to make and was not in your best interest. Those memories conjure up feelings of distaste, disdain, and even disgust. Integrity seems to be missing entirely in many of those interactions. Put into a vulnerable position, you feel like you were being taken advantage of. You don't want that to happen again. But, it does. It seems that this is the way the world works. Your experiences with manipulation have made a significant impression on how you think about the process of influencing. You are led to believe that in order to get your internal client to go along with your recommendations, or for people in your training programs to implement the strategies you share, you've got to blindly convince them that you are all-knowing and that you have every answer to their problems.

Some people believe they can use whatever means necessary to sway others to their position. They see influence as a win/lose proposition. This is the fastest way to turn others against you. People can tell when they're being manipulated.

Which experiences do you remember that were different than those where you felt manipulated? How did they leave you feeling?

In your encounters with others, you want them to feel good about having invested time meeting with you, not regretful.

Believe Influence Is Instant

If you're a coffee drinker, you're likely in the camp with others who swear by fresh brewed coffee. Why have establishments like Starbucks and Dunkin' Donuts become so popular? The barista is already brewing those fresh coffee beans before you walk in the door. You are anxious to get the freshest, most delicious cup of coffee possible, and you're willing to pay the price for it. Instant coffee can't possibly produce the same flavor. The coffee is processed, freeze dried, and ready for those times when you just need to add water, stir, and go. The flavor is tolerable but doesn't satisfy your palette the same way.

For some people, influence is like that. They think all it takes to succeed is standing in front of people and making their case.

Advertisers spend millions of dollars to persuade you to buy their products and services. They are buying impressions. Unique impressions are the number of individuals an advertiser is able to reach with a message. But they know that they can't effectively get their message across to you if you just see their advertisement once. That won't move you to buy. So, they purchase repeat impressions, giving them the opportunity to be in front of you multiple times so that you remember the message, feel a connection to their brand, and find a need or desire that their brand can fulfill for you. They also take some time to understand what will appeal to you, having an idea of what will best catch your attention and speak to you. The more it seems like they are speaking directly to you, the stronger the chance you will buy their products. Over time, they reach you even subconsciously. If their message speaks to you, you're ready to purchase.

The true test comes when you buy the product. How is your experience? Do they fulfill their promise from the advertisement? Does the product meet, and better yet, exceed your expectations? Are you compelled to buy the product again?

Once you have experience with one of the brand's products, you'll decide if you will purchase it again and try other products or services they offer.

Influence in our professional setting works in much the same way. The more someone knows you and has experience with you, the more influence you may be likely to have with them. People need repeated experiences with you. They will test not only the message, but also the messenger. What do they know about you? How do they feel about you? Are you trustworthy?

Treat Influence as a Transaction

Some people treat influence as if it's a transaction. Once you close the deal, your work is done. It has a clear end point, like the completion of a sale. The exchange takes place, and you move on. For example, you're in the market for a new car. You and the salesperson eventually negotiate the specific model and the terms of sale. You finally closed the deal! You drive off the lot toward home. The salesperson engages the next customer.

Influence, however, is more than a series of transactions. For example, at work, you have many of what seem like inconsequential interactions with your colleagues. You may be extra nice to a co-worker to get help on your IT support request ahead of others. You facilitated an engaging and productive workshop that received a favorable evaluation, but afterward you had little time for additional questions from participants. You might have failed to realize that though the initial "transaction" was complete, your ongoing ability to influence might be affected. You might believe that you can turn on the charm and get the same result. Your influence goes beyond your IT request or workshop. Influence takes time to build, develops across the encounters others have with you, and is extended as you build relationships.

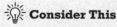 **Consider This**
How have any of these three mistakes been a barrier in your attempts to influence in the past?

Consequences of These Mistakes

These mistakes are common and easy to fall into. They are compelling. We prefer for our acts of influence to be painlessly quick and easy on our part. We get what we want and move on. When you focus on short-term gain, you have the potential to miss opportunities that may be longer term, richer outcomes.

Be careful that while you may look successful, your influence may not be as effective as you think. Such tactics may result in a temporary gain but lead to damaged relationships. The experience may leave others with feelings of embarrassment, frustration, disgust, and even anger.

Is it worth the risk?

Shift Your Perspective

To be a person of influence requires a shift in perspective about what influence is and how it works. Rather than a one-time act of manipulation, think of influence as a way of life. You influence others intentionally or unintentionally through words, action, language, and behaviors. Your sphere of influence is wider than you know. The fact is, we all observe and take cues from each other unconsciously.

Applying the principles described in the next chapters will enable you to avoid making these mistakes. Your reputation will precede you. And, you'll be able to combine the power of being a person of influence with a more appropriate approach to achieve an even more rewarding outcome.

Summary

Barriers to becoming a person of influence are heightened by three common mistakes. Manipulation will make you untrustworthy and can result in lasting relationship damage. Attempts at instant influence have shallow roots and can feel transactional and ingenuine. Shift your perspective about influence. It takes repeated positive experience with you to build the trust required for deeper influence. I offer a different approach to scale your influence effectiveness in chapter 4.

PART 2
Becoming Influential

CHAPTER 4

Becoming a Person of Influence

Tanisha realized that while she would need to coach Consuela on how best to influence Daniel, she also would be doing some influencing herself in the process. Her own skill at influence would be challenged.

There were several stakeholders with a hand in customer issues, from the C-suite to frontline employees, external partners, and customers themselves. Tanisha remembered that when she arrived as the organization's first talent development head, there was no one to show her around or teach her the ropes. An org chart didn't begin to explain to her all the ins and outs of relational politics and how she fit in. That first year, despite her sought-after coaching credential and industry experience, she almost quit. Twice. It wasn't until she became a regular at the new product lunch & learn that some of her colleagues even learned her name or what she did. So much for onboarding, she mused at the time. But over the years Tanisha had carved out a role for herself. When she hosted her own lunch & learn, she created teasers about her "product," which was people of course, impressing the attendees with what she knew about product developers and what they needed to do their own jobs.

Tanisha didn't want this customer service problem to grow beyond the three of them. And she knew it could. She could try to persuade Daniel of his own power to act as a positive force for the company, and not to simply react negatively, and with exhaustion, to the many requests that came his way. Consuela's problem wasn't the first, she could remind them, and wasn't going to be the last. This was an interconnected world, and as the company grew, there were going to be more of these frictions, not fewer. How would they handle the next one?

From her track record of being able to work collaboratively across the organization, Tanisha had grown a reputation of being a person of influence. She wanted to help not only Consuela, but also Daniel, see that they, too, were people of influence, with the ability to embody relational principles to scale their influence for any situation.

Influence as a Key Skill Across the Talent Development Profession

Supporting organizations and the professionals within them in becoming their best selves is why talent development professionals are so committed to their work. That takes influence. Though you can often see the potential in someone, they have to be able to see that potential and realize it within themselves. You can give people all the strategies and argue why a change in behavior or applying the hottest new tool will make all the difference. But you can't make them change or do it for them. Your best offense is to influence and inspire.

The importance of influence can be seen throughout the entire Talent Development Capability Model. Take a look and think about how influence can play out in each of the capabilities described in Figure 4-1. Keep these capabilities in mind as you continue to examine the facets of influence we're about to discuss in the rest of this chapter.

Whether early in your career or a seasoned professional, you have a need to communicate and influence across all levels of an organization. You most commonly influence at a peer level, where your daily interactions most frequently take place. You also have regular interactions with your direct manager and, sometimes less frequently, a level up with your boss's boss. You also work with external partners and customers on various projects.

Figure 4-1. The Talent Development Capability Model

Building Personal Capability	Developing Professional Capability	Impacting Organizational Capability
• Communication • Emotional Intelligence & Decision Making • Collaboration & Leadership • Cultural Awareness & Inclusion • Project Management • Compliance & Ethical Behavior • Lifelong Learning	• Learning Sciences • Instructional Design • Training Delivery & Facilitation • Technology Application • Knowledge Management • Career & Leadership Development • Coaching • Evaluating Impact	• Business Insight • Consulting & Business Partnering • Organization Development & Culture • Talent Strategy & Management • Performance Improvement • Change Management • Data & Analytics • Future Readiness

Do they see you as a person of influence? In what ways does influence play a role in your day-to-day responsibilities? Let's consider some examples:

You're considering a new learning management system and need to influence your peers on the leadership team to make the financial investment and allocate resources to the project.

With the sudden transition to remote work and virtual teams (which is expected to continue on a large scale into the future), the need for on-demand training, development, and resource accessibility has increased. Your analysis shows that the current system does not have the capability to handle the technical needs and anticipated volume, and does not connect to the recently updated human resources information system's talent management application. The company's ability to meet regulatory requirements on some of this training is at risk if the company doesn't make the transition. With competing priorities in other departments for the limited budget dollars available, selling this won't be so easy. You connect with some of your colleagues to determine how this new system would support the important priorities in their areas. Demonstrating concern for the best overall decision for the business at the time, you recommend potential options for consideration. People trust your judgment given the credibility you've built with other projects you've worked on together.

Changes in the industry will impact the future of your company's operations and talent needs. Talent development will need to play a critical role in the earliest stages of the scoping and planning process. You volunteer for the task force that is charged with understanding the opportunity, the effect on talent needs, and your company's response. Partnering with other departments, your team assesses what will be required to close skills gaps through talent reskilling and talent acquisition. You ensure that the team members who worked tirelessly under the short timeline have the opportunity to present the findings and recommendations.

Diversity, equity, and inclusion (DEI) has become a strategic priority for your organization. Talent development's role will be integral to leading this effort and influencing sustainable culture change. You suggest a diagnostic tool to evaluate the current state of DEI within the company. You know that not only data but also stories from associates across the company will illuminate the employee experience and needs. Others share your passion for creating a more inclusive culture. Engaging their support and advocacy will help get things moving in the right direction.

Your company is implementing a new accounting system and process in your organization. Some employees have been with the organization for years and are stuck in the mode of "this is the way we've always done things here." You're challenged with influencing culture and behavior change positively. You take the time to meet with individuals and groups to understand their concerns and get their input on needs for the new system. You invite involvement among different affected groups on both the committee that will evaluate potential options and the project team that will work on implementation.

You are designing a new training program for frontline new hires and need to gather information from subject matter experts. Employees feel like they have power when they have information and are seen as experts. They are reluctant to share their knowledge. How can you influence their perspective, demonstrating that sharing their knowledge to make the organization better as a whole is where their true power lies? You discover that they have limited opportunities to share their expertise. And when they do, they don't often get feedback on how it makes a difference. You ensure the information sharing on this project comes full circle, and that employees often overlooked are recognized for their contributions and value.

You're interviewing customers to learn more about their needs and how the company is serving them. You continue the interviews with employees in some of the customer-facing departments to help contextualize the feedback. You use this insight in discussions and decisions as you work as a business partner with other departments. Your willingness to gain firsthand knowledge from the front lines of the business earns you credibility. Your partnership, and potential for influence, deepens.

These are just a few examples of the multitude of daily opportunities you have to build influence with people across all areas of your organization. As you read through these, other examples likely came to mind. Through your talent development role, being a person of influence is an important role that brings with it a level of accountability. You have the potential to touch the heart and soul of individuals and organizations. Influence and how it is used matters. Your influence matters.

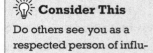

Consider This
Do others see you as a respected person of influence? Why or why not?

Growing Into Your Influence

The examples you just read demonstrate that you need a foundation of interpersonal skills, professional expertise, and organizational knowledge and savvy. Development in these capabilities will be instrumental in building credibility, trust, solid working relationships, and ultimately, your influence.

Interpersonal Skills and Influence

Interpersonal skills play a role in how you are able to connect with, show value for, and engage others, all of which are needed for influence. This quote commonly attributed to Theodore Roosevelt is a good reminder of the importance of human connection: "People don't care how much you know until they know how much you care."

In her role as director of organizational development, Vicky, a former client of mine, made it a point to get to know employees at all levels of the organization. Her employer was going through a busy couple of years—a major remodel, opening new venues, and, on top of all that, a devastating fire. Along with the extra workload came anxiety and frustration on many days. The empathy Vicky expressed in her interactions with others helped to build trust. She also championed the formation of employee committees that worked to develop wellness programs and support services to help her company work through the challenges on an individual, team, and organizational level.

Professional Expertise and Influence

Influence grows as you are able to apply your technical talent development knowledge and skills in a way that helps to maximize individual and organizational performance and potential. You serve as an expert in shaping talent development strategies that help ensure employees have the capability to meet ongoing organizational goals.

With the abrupt shift in remote work arrangements and processes, Doug, chief learning officer of a regional banking company, found himself having to reevaluate the new talent management process they were beginning to implement. He pulled his team together and reached out to some of his closest colleagues to assess how the needs were changing and explore potential solutions to meet them. The way teams worked together, the work processes, and the expectations of employees would continue to evolve for months to come. Doug was relieved that they didn't have to totally abandon their current plan, but did recommend some beneficial immediate adjustments. With them, he and his company were able to mitigate the concerns that had surfaced about how managers could best guide, support, and develop their teams in such an uncertain environment.

Organizational Knowledge and Influence

Influence at an organizational level focuses on gaining the knowledge, skills, and abilities needed to ensure talent development has a strategic seat at the table and is a partner in achieving business outcomes. Your knowledge of the industry and how the business operates, and your savvy in navigating organizational dynamics, enhance your potential for impact and perceived value. You align talent development initiatives with business priorities, are on the proactive side of enabling future organizational readiness, and are more effective at impacting operational results.

When Rita started a role in talent development with her new employer, she knew she had to quickly get up to speed to be seen as a business partner rather than an outsider. There were lots of acronyms and technical terms to learn in healthcare. She met with various people in different departments, attended meetings, and took advantage of the technical training that was available in order to learn everything she could. Her deep dive paid off. She was able to help strategize and communicate with staff in their professional language. In the process, she also discovered important business metrics and was able to align them for talent development in order to demonstrate business impact. That really got people's attention.

In each of these scenarios, these professionals were able to elevate their influence and level of impact. Influence is more than a skill. It is an enabler in your quest to become a highly valued talent development professional and leader.

 Consider This

In which capability area would you consider yourself to be strongest: interpersonal skills, professional expertise, or organizational knowledge and savvy? In what ways?

Influence: An Enabler

Seeking influence without authority is a position that talent development professionals often find themselves in as members of a support function. You need influence to enhance the effectiveness in your role. How do you obtain the level of influence that is required to get things done?

Jonathan Southgate (2018), an instructional designer and learning program manager, suggests that you already possess three advantages for greater influence:

- **Information power.** Leverage data to create compelling stories.
- **Expert power.** Own your value to apply your expertise in solving business problems.
- **Referent power.** Deeply understand the motivations and needs of your clients.

These advantages leverage the capabilities for growing your influence described in the previous section. The key is to recognize that these advantages exist and learn how to strategically use them in adding greater value.

When you combine these capabilities with the influence principles introduced in the next chapters, your overall influence has the potential to serve as an enabler.

Introducing the Influence With SCALE Principles

I would characterize the powerful principles introduced in this book as more of an influence value system. They are principles to live by and behaviors to adopt. The five principles of influence with SCALE come together in a framework that you can adopt personally and use to develop the skill within your organization.

Scale the effectiveness of your influence by focusing beyond tool selection and adopting these five powerful core relational principles. Allow them to become part of the fabric of who you are and how you operate. The principles are:

- **S: social capital.** These are dividends from the consistent investments you make in growing mutual, selfless relationships built on a foundation of empathy, genuine concern, respect, and trust.
- **C: courage.** Facing uncertainty, you are willing to take that step forward even though the road ahead is full of more questions than answers.
- **A: authenticity.** Guided by your values and principles, you are more self-aware and astutely conscientious and consistent in your interactions with others.
- **L: leaning in with passion.** You are invested in a meaningful purpose that inspires you to give your best effort.
- **E: engaging a diverse and inclusive workplace community.** You invite, welcome, and engage peoples' uniqueness to inspire an inclusive workplace community.

Each of the chapters that follow will dive deep into these principles for how to become a person of influence. I introduce you to the characteristics of each of these principles and guide you through steps you can take starting today to scale your influence for greater impact.

Are you ready?

Summary

Influence requires a foundation of interpersonal skills—your ability to interact with and engage others, professional expertise—knowledge and application of technical knowledge and skills, and organizational knowledge and savvy—business acumen and application. Integrating these capabilities with the five relational influence principles—social capital, courage, authenticity, lean in with passion, engage a diverse and inclusive workplace community—will scale your influence potential. You can begin to learn how in chapter 5.

CHAPTER 5

Social Capital

On a bright, sunny morning, Tanisha and Consuela left their offices and walked out of the building to a coffee shop down the street. It was a new, undiscovered place, and at mid-morning, they were unlikely to encounter colleagues.

Consuela made her way to a booth in the back as a man on the phone behind the counter motioned for Tanisha to help herself to the coffee pot sitting on the counter.

"Kind of a throwback place, I guess," Tanisha said as she sat down with their two cups. "Can't imagine they'll be making their money on coffee."

"It's the donuts," Consuela confided with an air of insider information. "My daughter raves about them. They're these amazing homemade confections they used to sell only online. Menu changes daily. This is their first storefront."

"Seriously? So why are we just drinking coffee?" Tanisha bolted out of the banquette and called to the man behind the counter, now off the phone. "Two of anything."

The man smiled. "Sprinkles or no?"

After they collected their food, Tanisha convinced Consuela to step back a bit, take a deep breath, and reset her approach to engaging Daniel about the customer service dilemma.

Tanisha was able to leverage her social capital with Consuela to persuade her to slow down and rethink the process. The two had worked together fairly regularly over Tanisha's six years at the company. As Consuela's team had various needs, Tanisha had partnered with them on talent acquisition, training and development, and updating talent management practices. The two have been successful work partners.

Consuela knew that she had to be more attentive to all that Daniel was dealing with first and not dump a whole new set of problems in his lap. They were in this together, and she had to demonstrate she meant that.

What Is Social Capital and Why Is It Important to Influence?

Social capital is the sum of the dividends from the consistent investments you make in growing mutual, selfless relationships built on a foundation of empathy, genuine concern, respect, and trust. Social capital is a relational asset that you build. The credibility you've earned from this intentional relationship building pays off when you need buy-in, assistance, or support. Social capital says we have something in the social bank account.

A social bank account works a lot like a financial bank account. For example, when my children were small, they'd think we could "just go to the money machine" to get money for whatever they wanted. Their Aunt Valerie would take them to the Dollar Store, which they called "the money store." To them, money grew on trees and you could go get as much as you wanted at any time. As adults, we know we are only able to take out what we put in. And, with a savings or investment account, the more you deposit in the account and the greater the interest rate, the more your investments will grow over time.

Social capital works in much the same way. You invest in a relationship with the expectation of growth. You make deposits to the relationship bank account and let those deposits grow. If you were to invest in a relationship just with the intention to ask for something in return, your relationship would be transactional, which has less relationship value. Relationships with social capital have deep relationship value. But if you do not take care to invest in your relationships, they will depreciate over time.

Trust grows over the course of building social capital. You have experience with a person, a track record that gives you an indication of their intention. When you have this type of equity in a relationship, influence is more likely.

"Influence comes in when you're respectful and you don't just come across sounding judgmental or disparaging about their opinions or their points of view. It's sitting down and having a conversation," says training and development expert Amy Shilliday in an interview for this book (2021).

Characteristics of Social Capital

Social capital comes from proactively investing in making real human connections with others. What are the key characteristics of social capital? Social capital encompasses value, selflessness, mutual respect and trust, and endurance. Let's explore each of these.

Value

A colleague and I are adjunct professors of project management with the University of Louisville College of Business. I have been an instructor of this course for several semesters. My colleague was preparing for her first semester of teaching this course during the COVID-19 pandemic. We were tasked with adapting the previously fully face-to-face course for hybrid instruction, which meant students had the choice of attending classes in-person or virtually. For a very interactive, hands-on course with lots of group work, there was a good amount of work ahead of us to transition our instruction for this course. We started with the materials I had previously used in my course section. Driven by our passion for our students, we collaborated using our years of experience in the field and met several times prior to and each week during the semester to prepare. We generated ideas for ensuring the course maintained its experiential delivery approach. We freely shared materials and resources. We were both truly invested in helping each other, producing the best course possible for our department and, most importantly, our students. In the process, we each also became better instructors.

People are more naturally drawn to associate with each other when there are common values, interests, and goals. There is some inherent value in the other person. Realizing value from the relationship is possible when there is a genuine investment in a beneficial relational outcome for both parties. The investment is not just toward achieving a transactional outcome. There is a perceived value of the individual and in the benefit that can be realized from knowing each other. Both parties are invested and contribute to adding value. You may not always be working on a specific project collectively, as my colleague and I were. You look out for what would be helpful for the other person and are glad to be a resource. You reach out to others on their behalf; you are a connector. They are willing to reach out to others on your behalf. You both add value.

Selflessness

When I was mid-career during my tenure at GE, I was asked to present an update during the annual leadership meeting. This was a big deal. The top executives of our division attended this meeting, with a goal of gaining alignment around key priorities for the year. I knew I had to be well prepared to deliver a compelling update. This presentation could make or break my chances to move up. I asked a trusted colleague for help.

She was all in. She found time for me during her work day, and even sacrificed some of her personal time to meet with me on a couple of weekends. We reviewed my material. She watched as I practiced my presentation for what seemed to be at least a hundred times. She was patient and generous with constructive feedback that helped me improve. As a result of the time she spent helping me, she ended up working some late evenings to get her own work done. Her approach to mentoring me through this process had an influence on me personally and professionally and strengthened the social capital in our working relationship. Her support and investment in me was priceless. The presentation went extremely well. My credibility and influence grew. Future opportunities opened to me to be able to present to this group again and to advance in my career.

Selflessness means that you have others' best interest at heart. Your intentions are not solely to take from the relationship, but to invest first and to invest willingly. You want to know a person for who they are, not just what they can do for you. I am not suggesting that you should expect to gain nothing from the relationship. And, there will be times when the need for a transactional interaction will be appropriate. What I am saying is that if you wish to influence, others will need to know you are not just trying to achieve your own agenda.

What's the impact of selfless behavior, and what makes someone potentially view your actions as selfless? Stefanie Johnson, a leadership authority and coach, describes how several CEOs stepped up when their organizations were going through times of crisis. "Leader self-sacrifice," she writes, "caused employees to feel more positively toward their leaders and more committed to the organizations during crises" (Johnson 2020). CEOs of companies such as LinkedIn, Citigroup, Bank of America, FedEx, Marriott International, Delta, and Uber committed to cutting their own salaries, or not laying off employees, during the COVID-19 pandemic.

Why did Johnson find these examples of self-sacrifice to be most effective? First of all, these leaders were willing to sacrifice right along with the sacrifices their employees were having to make. And their sacrifices were significant. Secondly, their sacrifices were purposeful. My former employer, like so many others, switched their factories to producing personal protective equipment (PPE) and ventilators during the pandemic. Finally, Johnson says it's important to be aggressively transparent about how the dollars or output from the sacrifice are being redirected—not for personal glory, but to build trust that the intention was genuine. For example, the salary cut of the CEO of one of my clients was redirected to fund employee grants during the crisis.

There's ample opportunity to be selfless outside of a crisis, as well, as in the example of my colleague who helped me in preparing for my leadership presentation. You have to be aware and open to those opportunities.

Mutual Respect and Trust

I'm sometimes asked to work with teams that are experiencing conflict. The work environment is stressful, and productivity and quality of work suffer as a result. Little social capital exists within these teams. When meeting with those involved during my initial discovery interviews, concerns over the levels of respect or trust are often surfaced. In what ways are these important relationship values broken? Someone creates a story in their head about a colleague's intentions and alliances, and they act on those assumptions. What is shared is not always held in confidence. Misaligned priorities create competition. Junior level staff feel invisible, as their opinions and ideas are often overlooked. There's a focus on self and survival rather than working together toward contributing their best work.

To recreate a functional, high-performing team, my work with teams in conflict often begins with addressing what is sabotaging basic human respect and trust. As we remove some of the misunderstandings and insecurities, realign values, and rediscover value in each other, we work on opening lines of communication. Relationships begin to rebuild and, over time, respect and trust develop.

Contrast these groups with other high-performing teams I work with, and what stands out are examples of selfless investments toward providing support and in developing and growing each individual and the team as a whole.

Both respect and trust are foundational to building social capital. Respect and trust are both earned and given.

Respect is defined as "esteem for or a sense of the worth or excellence of a person, a personal quality or ability" (Dictionary.com, nd). You hold someone is high regard first for their value as a human being. Then respect will further develop as other factors such as a person's values and character are revealed. Respect demonstrates that I value you for who you are. You give respect and behave in a respectable manner to earn respect in return.

In his book, *The Trust Edge* (2011), author David Horsager refers to trust as "a confident belief in someone or something. It is the confident belief in an entity to do what is right, to deliver what is promised, and to be the same every time, in spite of the circumstances. Trust speaks to being reliable, dependable, and capable."

Colleagues are drawn to you when you have a reputation of high integrity and character, one that you have demonstrated to them that they can trust. When there is trust, people value and come to you for your opinion. They care about what you have to say because you genuinely care about them, in turn.

Endurance

My husband loves to garden. Our lawn is a lush carpet of grass, filled with beautiful perennials—roses, lilies, banana trees, crepe myrtles, and more! He waters, weeds, and fertilizes the plants. He cuts back the plants in the fall in preparation for the winter. He nurtures his garden so that, regardless of the cold, snow, and lack of rain, it will be a vibrant oasis of color through the spring and summer year in and year out.

Like a garden meticulously cared for, professional relationships with social capital stand the test of time. Coordinating various market research projects was part of my responsibilities in various roles across my corporate career. Our company had a long-standing relationship with a research company who knew our business and industry well. A new market research professional, Susan, joined the research company. She was deeply experienced in the market research industry and worked to quickly learn our business and industry. Having worked together on many research projects, she became a trusted partner. Even as both our careers took different paths over the years, we made it a point to stay in touch and get together for lunch from time to time. I've engaged Susan with some of my other clients and reached out to her for research advice for my own company. I've had the opportunity to reciprocate with informal coaching around her career. We respect, trust, and care about each other as friends and professionals. The social capital that began to develop years ago endures today.

Social capital deepens from the experiences others have with you over time. Time provides multiple opportunities for interaction and for demonstrating the value in the relationship. When you plant seeds in a flower garden, the flowers don't bloom immediately. Likewise, a relationship must be nurtured over time in order for it to grow. When a relationship is tested, because of the value, selflessness, respect, and trust that it is rooted in, you can withstand the challenges that are sure to arise.

Steps to Scale Your Social Capital

These three steps are key to scaling your social capital:
1. Reach out.
2. Selflessly add value.
3. Build respect and trust.

Reach Out

Get out of the nest! Be proactive in reaching out to connect with people periodically. You get so busy that it's easy to sit at your desk or computer. Or, you're running to meetings all day. That leaves you little time to have a meaningful conversation with the people you do see or to connect intentionally with people you rarely see.

As a talent development professional, your role often requires you to interact with others in the organization, whether to determine development needs, do research toward improving talent management policies and practices, or facilitate training. Take those opportunities to get to know people. Check on colleagues who have been in your training sessions to see how they are doing and follow up on the progress they have made on implementing what they learned.

Reach out to people periodically to say hello and inquire about what's new and interesting in their world. Send a brief email, text, instant message, or make a quick call. Use a social media platform to share a resource such as an article or report that would be beneficial to them. As your social capital builds through such interactions, you create even more opportunities for interacting.

Through this approach, I have developed social capital with someone whom I have actually never met in person. Iana and I initially met when she contacted me about speaking for her professional association. From that conversation, we agreed to schedule another call where we could get to know each other better professionally and personally. We discovered common interests, professional experiences, and career goals. We try to reach out periodically with a quick call or email to check in. Iana has become a trusted colleague and friend through these interactions.

Be genuinely curious about others. Don't let small talk be a waste of time. Small investments of time can return exponentially. It's in such discussions that we begin to find common interests and a foundation of mutuality. You demonstrate that your interest goes beyond the transactional needs of your jobs.

Selflessly Add Value

To add relationship value requires you to be selfless. Selflessness requires empathy and a genuine concern for others. Empathy is being able to put yourself in the other person's shoes so you can better relate to them. When you have empathy rather than being judgmental, a person you are communicating with is more willing to open up to you. Empathy communicates to the other person that "I see you" and "I care about how you're feeling and what you may be going through." Empathy doesn't show up as trying to give advice or fix the concerns of others. Empathy requires listening nonjudgmentally.

When you have a genuine concern for others, it becomes much easier to be selfless and to build social capital. The focus is less on you and more on others. If a relationship is building social capital, both parties are selfless. You open doors and support each other in achieving your greatest potential.

In "The Joint Effects of Personality and Workplace Social Exchange Relationships in Predicting Task Performance and Citizenship Performance," Dishan Kamdar and Linn Van Dyne (2007) explain that "social exchange theory and the norm of reciprocity describe social exchange as an open-ended stream of transactions, with both exchange partners making contributions and receiving benefits. These exchanges are open ended because the form and timing of contributions is discretionary. Social exchange contrasts with economic exchange, which specifies exchanges on a quid pro quo basis."

To add value, you need to be aware of what would be of value to others. Peter Demarest (2020), a leading pioneer in the science of neuro-axiology, states that "value is the degree to which something can enhance quality of life." How do you know what someone else may value? Be observant in your interactions. What are important priorities in their work and life? Where do they tend to spend their time and energy? Ask them what their needs or interests are. What would be helpful for them? Have a genuine interest in getting to know, understand, relate to, and help others. Engage with genuine curiosity about who people are and what they care about, seeking to find common values and interests from which your relationship can begin to develop. Listen empathetically to understand others' points of view. You listen not only to their words, but also tune into their body language and tone when they are communicating verbally and nonverbally via email or text. Remove distractions so that you can really lean in.

Your focus is on understanding what others need and how to be a resource. You make deposits in the relationship before asking for anything. Your motives are not "give to get." You've gotten calls from the people who only reach out when they need something. Don't be that person. When you contribute with true compassion, good will return to you.

"Influence comes down to Covey's fifth habit, seek first to understand and then to be understood," says Amy Shilliday. "And it really is about listening. When I think about influence, it's not just lobbying your ideas or what you want. It's really learning whatever the other person's—or the organization you're working with—needs and struggles are and applying a practice, behavior, or tool in a way that's going to be more meaningful for them."

Inquire about how you can help and be willing to assist based on what you are able to do. Set clear expectations with each other. Share ideas and resources that are pertinent to what you've learned about them. Be a connector by introducing people to one another inside and outside of work.

A good deed is often repaid. Even though your motive isn't to add value to get something in return, a person is likely to feel obligated to also do something for you. "People will help if they owe you for something you did in the past to advance their goals. That's the rule of reciprocity." says Robert Cialdini (2007), whose six principles of influence we discussed in chapter 2. In this case, reciprocity is not merely a transactional or economic exchange, it is a goodwill exchange that has the potential to strengthen the relationship.

Build Respect and Trust

In your daily interactions with others, whether formal and informal, you want to be mindful of how you engage. Do you value and show respect for others? How you interact and work with others affects social capital development, which in turn can impact the effectiveness of your work, their work, and your work environment overall.

"A high proportion of collegial and special peer relationships may be indicative of an organization in which employees like one another, get along well, and help each other out," explains Patricia Sias in her 2009 book, *Organizing Relationships*. Her study of research on workplace relationships revealed that employees were more motivated to interact with each other and became closer when perceptions of similarity and liking were present. Similarities may involve aspects such as demographics, attitudes, an enjoyment of each other's personalities, or employment status. "Peers who worked in close physical proximity (e.g., had desks, offices, or work stations near each other) or who worked on projects together were also more likely to become friends," Sias adds. Her findings are in line with Cialdini's influence research, as he discovered liking to be an important persuasion principle.

"Within organizations, people have to see each other as human beings or there will be no social glue," explains John M. Gottman, executive director of the Relationship Research Institute, during his interview with Harvard Business Review senior editor Diane Coutu (2007). When we truly value others as human beings, respectful relationships have the potential to form. Valuing others begins with getting to know them.

Much of our perceived social standing is derived from the respect we receive, which becomes a cue that signals others. An example is when respect comes with a person's position. We are often taught as we grow up to show respect to people with authority. We honor the position. Credence is given to the person because of the position they hold. If the individual acts in a way that is congruent with their position, we dutifully show a certain level of respect. We expect the person to uphold the characteristics that are associated with the position. As you observe them and have interactions with them, you expect consistency.

Positional respect does not deepen social capital. Social capital grows with experience with the individual. You may not have any interactions with a leader that would allow you to know them beyond a surface level. However, the decisions they make and actions they take impact you. And their selfless acts make a more personal connection. Your respect for them and the social capital they hold from you may grow or decline as a result. You are determining the social capital the leader has with you. Social capital is shallow in this one-sided, transactional type of exchange. They may hold no social capital with you because they don't know you or have had no experience with you. When leaders reach out beyond their inner circle to the front line of the organization to connect with employees, they get to know who people are. Mutual respect and trust can develop on a more human, rather than positional, level.

Kristie Rogers's research on respect reveals that two types of respect are valued by employees in the workplace: owed respect, extended to you because you are a member of a group or organization, and earned respect, extended to individuals based on their perceived value. "Owed respect," she describes, "meets the universal need to feel included. It's signaled by civility and an atmosphere suggesting that every member of the group is inherently valuable" (2008). Rogers further explains that "earned respect recognizes individual employees who display valued qualities or behaviors. It distinguishes employees who have exceeded expectations and, particularly in knowledge work settings, affirms that each employee has unique strengths and talents. Earned respect meets the need to be valued for doing good work."

Creating social capital through respect must go beyond a recognition of a person's position or owed respect to a deeper level of valuing and appreciating the essence of an individual's character and recognized contributions. Those contributions are investments in the relationship, as well as to the organization.

Respect is earned and given. If you want people to respect you, you have to be worthy of respect. You have to give respect first before respect can be received. You come to respect someone more as you have experienced them. Respect is demonstrated to others through honoring their value by the way you treat them. Are you mannerly? Do you listen openly and nonjudgmentally to what they have to say? Do you treat others in a way that values who they are?

Respect sends a signal that people have social worth; it is an important feedback mechanism and catalyst for their professional growth.

Trust also is earned and given. Social capital develops through what corporate L&D leader Jimmy Nelson refers to as "unconditional trust building" (2021). You've earned the right to be trusted by following through on your commitments, maintaining confidentiality, and demanding respect for others by following the rule of being loyal to the absent, which Stephen R. Covey reminds us of in his book, *The 7 Habits of Highly Effective People* (1989).

Think about the people who influence you most. They are the people who have the greatest social capital with you. You know something about them. You've come to trust their opinion. You know they are genuine because they have been consistent. They've demonstrated that they are trustworthy. People are more likely to listen to and follow others when there is trust.

When trust is extended to others, it opens the door for trust to be extended in return. How people treat each other sends a signal about whether their trustworthiness is questioned. When people trust each other in the workplace, teamwork, communication, and productivity are strong. And when conflicts arise within teams, they are better able to resolve them.

The importance of trust in the work environment also is reflected in psychologist Douglas McGregor's X-Y motivation theory. Managers' attitudes around trust set the tone for the culture of an organization. McGregor explains that Theory X managers distrust workers, believing that they are self-centered and only motivated to work in support of their fundamental physiological needs (air, food, water, to be able to provide basic needs for their family) and safety needs (having a secure job and a safe work environment), the first two levels of Maslow's hierarchy of needs. They dislike their work and lack accountability and initiative. Theory Y managers, on the other hand, trust workers. They believe that, given appropriate working conditions, most people are self-motivated to do a good job, will take responsibility, and show initiative. These managers recognize employees are motivated across all levels of Maslow's hierarchy of needs, and they are active partners in helping them achieve self-actualization. These attitudes are demonstrated in managers' behaviors and have a ripple effect across employee relationships. How people work together and the morale within an organization are telling of the trust that is present.

In what ways can talent development professionals build trust in their relationships and inspire trust within their organizations? Like Theory Y managers, extending trust begins by assuming others' intentions are honorable, and ensuring yours are, as well. Earn trust by taking the steps we've already discussed in this chapter: Reach out to make genuine connections with others, selflessly add value, and build respect. Trust, too, is often found in the little things you do in your interactions with others, such as following through on your commitments. Share information instead of believing there is power in holding it to yourself. Be honest and avoid sharing untruths. Be willing to take responsibility for mistakes. And apologize when your words or actions have been hurtful, whether intentionally or not.

 Consider This

Consider one of your professional relationships. How have these characteristics played a role in the development and deepening of social capital?
- Value
- Selflessness
- Mutual respect and trust
- Endurance

Scale Your Social Capital

Social capital is essential across an organization for meaningful and productive working relationships to exist. In a workplace where relationships have a foundation of social capital, there are greater opportunities for positive influence.

Much of the work of talent development professionals is based around the relationships they develop. Take the lead on making the investments in those relationships so that social capital develops and deepens over time. The characteristics of social capital align well with the purpose of talent development and the work you are charged with every day. You add value by selflessly designing and implementing initiatives that enhance the potential within individuals, teams, and organizations. People are more open to your partnership when respect is demonstrated and trust is earned. Scale your influence through social capital.

Summary

In the workplace, the decisions you make and actions you take often impact other people. The concern you have about what that impact will be on others can add to or detract from the social capital held for you. When you demonstrate a willingness to selflessly add value for the mutual benefit of others, social capital has the opportunity to positively develop and grow. From that social capital, because there is trust from reliable experiences with you, a deeper level of influence is possible. Influence emerges not just from what you say or any particular action, but because of the respect and regard for you as a person of influence. When a foundation of social capital exists, the courage that may be required at times may be less difficult to draw upon. We'll explore this idea further in the next chapter.

CHAPTER 6

Courage

Tanisha had encouraged Consuela to build on the social capital she had with Daniel. The two women had discussed the current challenges of organization growth affecting them all and the disruptions to Daniel's supply-chain operations. With the speed of technology advancements, the company had expanded into new industries, competitiveness had increased, and speed to market was becoming more critical. More new products than usual had been introduced in the past six months. Supply chain had to expand their capacity to get more products delivered to more customers and build in new systems to support the complexities this introduced.

From Daniel's perspective, everything was going pretty well. Consuela's team was experiencing the cracks in the operations that may not have been so evident to Daniel. Getting him to partner with Consuela would take some work. Daniel was convinced that Consuela only had to hire more people. Consuela had already added and onboarded new staff based on the plan he supported. She wasn't so sure adding more people would be more than a temporary bandage. She would have to make the case for other potential root causes.

Consuela dreaded interactions with Daniel. They were very stressful. She would need to have her game plan together and confidently make her case. At times, she felt it might be easier to just deal with her problems by herself as best she could, without involving Daniel at all.

Consuela wanted to make sure she had been thorough in examining the improvement opportunities within her team to avoid further conflict with Daniel. Maybe she could try retraining her team. Consuela approached Tanisha about additional training.

But Tanisha had met with the instructional designers and facilitators assigned to the initial training, reviewed the evaluations, and met with the customer service team. She also reviewed Consuela's customer service data. Tanisha had no choice but to conclude that the initial training had accomplished its goal. The next step would be uncovering and resolving the supply-chain operational issues with Daniel.

Tanisha knew this was not what Consuela wanted to hear. The additional training would help Consuela show that she was taking some action within her own department. But Tanisha believed neither training nor adding more staff would make any measurable improvement in solving these issues for customers at this stage. As the supply-chain issues were resolved down the road, there could be a need to train the team on updates, and they could revisit it then. Tanisha really wanted to help Consuela but would need to remain confident in her conclusions that training at this stage was not advised and be courageous in communicating that. She would also need to equip Consuela to courageously carry this same message forward to Daniel.

Tanisha walked through the details and rationale with Consuela, who reluctantly agreed that training was not the answer. Now, they needed to approach Daniel. How should they do it?

Before Consuela's first meeting with Daniel, she met with Tanisha to prepare. They considered different ways Daniel could respond and had additional information ready if needed. Tanisha suggested they meet with one of the directors who worked closely with Daniel to provide some additional insight.

Consuela was anxious going into the meeting with Daniel. She expected pushback, but she felt well prepared and confident in the data and her conclusions.

After two intense meetings, Daniel and Consuela came to an agreement on what some of the contributing issues were in both departments and began to map out a plan for how to work together to resolve them. Selling the plan to senior leaders to get the budget would take a little political maneuvering. That would be the next challenge.

What Is Courage and Why Is It Important to Influence?

Do you remember the first time you jumped off the diving board into the swimming pool? You were a good swimmer but had to build up the courage to be willing to take that step. Would you be strong enough to swim out of the deep end of the pool? Would the water rush into your nose? You felt a rush of adrenaline as you jumped, a huge relief as you splashed into the water, and excitement as you swam to the side of the pool and ran back over to the ladder to jump again.

Courage is facing uncertainty and being willing to take that step forward even though you're scared and the road ahead is full of more questions than answers. Courage requires you to dig deep into your heart and soul in order to get to a place of readiness. Courage is the "mental or moral strength to venture, persevere, and withstand danger, fear, or difficulty," and stems from the Latin root word "cor," which means heart (*Merriam-Webster's Dictionary*).

Vincent van Gogh asked: "What would life be if we had no courage to attempt anything?"

Fear is a natural part of being human and must be present for you to have courage. Fear is not all bad, especially as it compels you to make a move toward change. Courage requires fear. If you are courageous, fear still exists, but does not overwhelm you. "Courage is not the absence of fear but rather the commitment of one to overcome it," writes leadership expert and coach Tameka Williamson (2018).

Having courage means you're willing to step out and become vulnerable, feeling rather uncomfortable, less confident in your abilities, and uncertain about what the outcome will be. You thoughtfully and attentively push on anyway, toward the diving board, even when you'd rather stay where it's more comfortable, floating around in the shallow end of the swimming pool.

The need for and demonstration of courage are frequently present in talent development. You're supporting while pushing the organization to go beyond its current state. That requires challenging the status quo, encouraging change, and actively preparing the organization for the future. This is not always a popular position to be in. Not everyone is ready for the change, nor do they agree on the path to getting there. Remain where it's comfortable, however, and neither you nor the organization will grow.

"We do our best to inspire a change in behavior in others when, ultimately, it depends on their willingness to take action," reflects Sandi Maxey. "We don't really control that and must have the courage to say our intervention may or may not work given the commitment of those involved."

You sometimes may be in the minority in your opinion or ideas. There are times when your opinions and recommendations may be called into question. It can feel like the organization's and your personal values are being questioned. So often you want to please others and feel pressured to show you're being supportive by following through on exactly what was asked of you. You will need to be courageous in doing what you believe is right or, at times, even defending your position.

As a talent development professional, which of these situations requiring courage have you experienced?

- Making a recommendation you believe is right when it wasn't specifically what was asked for.
- Being honest with developmental feedback and praise.
- Advising that training or talent development are not the solution for a problem.
- Sharing your thoughts and perspectives when they don't go along with the group (avoiding group think).
- Advocating for a talent development solution when others are pushing back.
- Designing a workshop or training material to inspire a change in the behavior of others.
- Presenting your ideas verbally or in writing, making your thoughts and beliefs public.

- Facilitating a training session that guides others to new ideas and perspectives.
- Being honest about what talent development methods can or can't deliver.
- Being willing to risk failure by being innovative and trying new talent development solutions.
- Challenging cultural norms, going outside of "this is how we do things here."

What was most challenging for you in being able to demonstrate courage in these situations? How did you work through the challenges? How was your influence impacted?

To be courageous does not mean you are stepping out blindly. Courage comes from being prepared, having a plan or action steps to follow, at least for the initial stages. You've carefully contemplated whether or not you should take action and what that step forward should be. This more thoughtful approach to being courageous is what business professor and author Kathleen Reardon (2007) refers to as the "courage calculation: a method of making success more likely while avoiding rash, unproductive, or irrational behavior." This puts you in a better position to be of influence. Winging it rarely works. When you've given thought to what you should do, what you should say, and how you move forward, you can be more reflective—asking yourself if this accomplishes what you hope—and adjust if necessary.

To be courageous thoughtfully and attentively is especially important in the workplace. You want to be conscientious of the impact on your reputation and the social capital you have developed in your working relationships. Being alienated is not the result you want. You need the ability to get things done in your role in the future, and getting things done requires the support and collaboration of others.

When you refuse to give in to fear, doors open to reaching your full potential and using that potential to be of influence toward positive change within your organization.

Characteristics of Courage

What can Disney fairytales and superhero movies teach us about courage? In these action drama stories, the focus is on the courage of the main character, the protagonist, to overcome the villain. They are usually the most unlikely character to face the villain and overcome adversity. The story typically unfolds as they attempt to find the courage to do what is needed to save the day. They become the heroine or hero.

What is your favorite fairytale or superhero character? Which of the following characteristics of courage do you find to be common in those stories?

Courage Found in Ordinary People

These superheroes are not the most popular or confident persons as they go about day to day. Most people around them don't know that they possess the power or courage within them to take on the toughest challenges. They may be faced with a situation where they have to fight to save their lives or the lives of those around them, even though they didn't choose to play that role or don't believe they had the power to do so.

There may be many situations at work where you don't feel like you are in the position to speak up. "Who would listen to you?" you might ask.

Kyle was in a meeting where most people were at higher levels in the organization than he was. The conversation about the new employee orientation program seemed to be going on around him rather than with him. But he had data on employee turnover from the analysis his boss asked him to do, but hadn't brought up, that needed to be shared and discussed before a decision was made. He felt that the data might alter the group's direction. He sat there contemplating if, when, and how he should interject. Cautiously, Kyle asked if he could share some information that could be helpful. All eyes were on him. The information he shared brought new insights into the discussion.

"Most acts of courage don't come from whistleblowers or organizational martyrs. Instead, they come from respected insiders at all levels who take action because they believe it is the right thing to do . . . And when they manage the process well, they don't necessarily pay a high price for their actions; indeed, they may see their status rise as they create positive change," explains professor and author James Detert (2018).

Worth Fighting For

We are not called to be courageous when the path ahead is easy. Courage builds from facing adversity. There has to be a challenge to overcome to grow. Growth comes from being challenged and getting through the challenge, albeit sometimes with scars from the battles faced. "Courage is the will to act in spite of fear or despair for the purpose of human growth," explains leadership expert and author Catherine Perme (2016b).

Along the journey toward prevailing over a challenge, you will experience setbacks and disappointments. To emerge victorious requires coming face to face with core values and beliefs to discover their truth and their strength.

Perme writes that "fostering organizational courage is difficult but the key lies in being true to vision and values while at the same time embracing current reality, despair, and fears."

Stepping up to be courageous is difficult. The prize or outcome on the other side of the adversity must be valuable compared to the risk. Otherwise, it's a lot easier to walk away. And with little at stake, the reward is inconsequential.

Roberta knew that many of the employees in the organization were afraid of the changes that were coming in their organization. Job skills were shifting, which meant people may be at risk of losing their jobs. Roberta approached her peers about making investments in retraining workers to retain as many current employees as possible. She knew that would not be a popular option, given the tight budget dollars and priorities for investing in innovation and new technology. But it would be an investment with rewards in the short and longer term. A lot of the decisions had already been made. She thought, though, it was important enough to the organization's success and to her personal values to try to generate some support around this effort.

Determining the importance of your goal is one of the important components of what Kathleen Reardon (2007) calls the "courage calculation." In determining the importance of the goal, Reardon suggests considering the consequences of doing something versus doing nothing, the urgency of the situation, the degree to which the situation should be elevated, the alignment with your personal values, and even considering the effect on your career. "Courage," she adds, "is not about squandering political capital on low-priority issues."

Vulnerability Demonstrates Strength

When you step out to take a risk, you can't anticipate everything that will happen. The journey to the outcome is uncertain and likely to be bumpy. We all want to win, to be right, to have things go our way. The uncertainty of how things will turn out puts you in a vulnerable position.

Especially in the early stages of the story, superheroes do not face their challenges with perfection and are not always successful. They often come out of those initial battles with bumps and bruises, hurt feelings and egos. Sometimes it requires going back to the drawing board, taking a rest, building up their physical and mental strength, or consulting with their partners or a wise advisor on how to proceed.

They take note of how they were most challenged in those battles and work on their areas so that they are better prepared the next time. And, there's still some level of fear they have to overcome. But they come back stronger than before.

In the workplace, when you stick your neck out and take a risk, you're concerned about the consequences if things don't go as well as you had hoped. It's natural to try to protect your ego and reputation by deflecting blame, or by not even taking the risk at all.

Nancy was facilitating a two-day training on a new process for installing equipment at customer sites. Participants were colleagues across the company who were at about the same point in their careers as she. During the training, a few of the participants challenged the new process. It was very different than their current process and would take longer to complete until they had more experience under their belt. Nancy was afraid this might happen. She knew the sensitivities around the new process but didn't really address them. She tried to convince participants that this new process was much better if they'd just give it a try. The first day of training ended with a lot of tension and not much accomplished. She was quite frustrated and concerned about her credibility among her peers, but knew she had to rebuild their trust in her or the whole training would be a waste of everyone's time. At the start of training the next day, Nancy admitted that she was not being very open and asked the group to share their concerns and ideas. She promised to take that information back to the department manager for reconsideration.

The key, writes author and speaker Margie Warrell (2021), is "Work to get it right, not to be right."

Rarely a Single-Handed Feat

In these superhero stories, though the weight falls on the main character's shoulders to fight the villain, they are usually not alone. There's usually another character, an ally, who befriends them, advises them, and either knowingly or unknowingly helps them through the challenge. There are people in their circle who help lift their confidence and are right there with them through the struggles. Some play a physical role in facing the challenge; others play a strategic or emotional support role.

Nancy successfully persuaded colleagues in her installation training workshop to provide more detail around their ideas for how to improve the installation process. They became allies in their campaign to lobby the department manager to reconsider procedures. Alone, either party might not have been able to get the attention of the decision makers or demonstrate the importance of the needed changes.

Work rarely gets done alone in the workplace. You need the input or involvement of others to be productive and effective in achieving goals.

Ready for Battle

The most courageous superheroes have prepared for this time, with strategy and the right tools to get the job done. They are equipped with what they need to have a shot at prevailing. Though they may have been born with superpowers or were chosen to have those powers from some event in their lives, they had to practice and learn how to use, manage, and apply their powers responsibly.

Samuel would be facilitating his first training workshop since he joined the company. Though he was nervous, he felt prepared. He had completed a key certification and had experience in facilitation at his previous company. He mapped out a detailed plan for the full-day workshop and practiced a number of times in preparation. Being new to the company, he wasn't sure he fully understood the context of all the material. He met with subject matter experts from a few departments to learn more about the organization. Being courageous can be less ominous when you know you are well equipped for the task at hand.

Confident, but Not Overconfident

Confidence, a strong belief that you can overcome adversity, is essential. In these superhero stories, the characters believed they could do something to make a difference. They knew the battle they faced would be tough. But they prepared themselves and had others in their corner to encourage and partner with them.

Samuel had the experience and had well prepared to facilitate his first training workshop. He could feel confident that he was ready. But he also was aware of where his vulnerabilities were. Being new to the company, he still had a lot to learn. He wanted to make sure he remained humble in his approach to leading the workshop and engaging with the employees.

When you have confidence, you have a strong, yet realistic, belief in what you are able to accomplish. However, when you are overconfident, you may overestimate your abilities or just assume the outcome is going to go your way. Pride can get in the way. You may find yourself feeling that you don't need to prepare. You've got this. That's when failure is imminent and can hurt the most.

 Consider This
- What has been one of the most challenging situations in your career that required courage?
- In what ways did you demonstrate courage?
- How was your influence impacted?
- What did you learn about yourself from that experience?

Steps to Scale Your Courage

Sometimes you see others acting courageously and think, "That could never be me." What's the key? "In business, courageous action is really a special kind of calculated risk taking," writes Reardon (2007). "Business courage . . . is a skill acquired through decision-making processes that improve with practice."

Courage can be learned and developed with practice and experience. That's good news.

These three steps can guide you in how to scale your courage for deeper influence:

1. Embrace the challenge.
2. Reduce the risk with preparation.
3. Don't go it alone.

Embrace the Challenge

We don't like it when we're challenged. We prefer for our journey in this life to be void of obstacles. But, that's not reality.

A firefighter sometimes has to go into the burning house in order to fight a fire successfully. Running into the flame is the most dangerous, but sometimes most productive way to get the fire under control so it can eventually be extinguished.

You often face adversity as you fulfill your purpose in your day-to-day responsibilities. It may be that others don't agree with your recommendations. Others may not have the same priorities and don't view your initiatives at the same level of importance. You may not have the resources you believe are adequate. But you have a vision for what is possible. Influence will be required to get to that outcome, along a journey that takes work, time, and courage.

Management scholar and psychoanalyst Manfred F.R. Kets de Vries (2020) describes courage as a muscle that you can develop and practice: "The more we are able to face our fears, the more we will replace fear-based responses with courageous ones."

Your first step toward discovering courage is to embrace the fact that there is a challenge to work through. Know that you can get through it, even without magic powers. You are enough.

James, a talent development professional, was asked to be on the transition team for the upcoming company merger. He was assigned to the committee that would identify talent needs and staffing requirements. James was fairly new to the team, which had already been meeting for several weeks. In attending the weekly meetings, James was doing a lot of listening and learning about the situation and the needs assessment that had been completed. He was also observing the dynamics of the group. The committee comprised team members from both merging companies and was chaired by Roger, a leader from the other company. The team members from Roger's company seemed to be most vocal and taking most of the lead on things. During discussions, there was a lot of agreement, as if everyone was expected not to challenge what had been presented. Rarely did people raise objections or concerns. In one meeting, they were considering how the next steps in the talent assessment process would work. James had some questions and, knowing their organization, had some ideas for how best to go about the assessment process. As soon as he spoke up, he knew his comments were not welcome and began to back off. James knew it would be difficult to get the group to be open to his input.

When you're facing a situation that is difficult or uncomfortable, instead of pushing it away, study it, understand it the best you can, and decide you're going to find a way through it rather than allowing it to diminish you. Embrace the challenge. Here's how:

Assess What You're Dealing With

Take some time to do a reality check so that you can assess what you're dealing with, how important the concern is to address, and what level of attention it may need. And, be aware of how your emotions may be influencing your perspectives and decisions. The following questions can guide your reflections:

- What are the facts?
- Is this really important?
- What's the worst possible thing that could happen? (Often the worst is that you do nothing, and the challenge only gets bigger.)
- What is the best possible result for all involved?
- What steps can you take to get to that point?
- How might your personal and organizational values influence your decisions and actions?

Use the insights to determine if and how you might proceed.

Roger, the talent and staffing committee leader, was pretty emphatic about following the assessment process as he had laid it out. The easier path would be for James to go along with the current plan and hope for the best. But James cared more about making sure the new team got this right for the benefit of employees. Their decisions would impact people's jobs and livelihoods. And if the company staffing was not adequately aligned, the company's operations post-merger would be constrained. James had to figure out how to get Roger and the team to consider the implications of the current plan more broadly. He also had to decide if this was something he wanted to go against Roger on. He didn't want to risk the social capital and trust they would build coming out of this work together, which could be important for his career.

James did some additional investigating to ensure he understood all possible angles of the current plan and could be objective. He also needed to understand the politics of the committee, who the players were, their relationships, the power dynamics in the group, and the history of how the group dysfunction evolved. From there, he would be better informed before deciding what action he would take, if any.

"Choose your battles. Assess whether engaging in a potential battle—whatever the outcome might be—is likely to aid or hinder in winning the war," notes James Detert (2018).

Set Realistic Expectations

Given the realities, what should the expectations be for yourself and others involved? What do you believe the outcomes will be from taking courageous action? Sometimes you have very high expectations going out the gate, expecting that you'll reach your goal easily. But that might not be reasonable. Trial and error might be required.

Do have high expectations of yourself and stretch yourself beyond where you might feel comfortable. But, balance that with what you learn from your reality check. Use that information to guide your decision making and planning, not as an excuse to remain comfortable. Change your goal from avoiding mistakes to asking yourself, "With the information I have right now, what are the risks? What do I believe would be the best next step? What might be the result of taking that next step?" Give yourself some grace, knowing that everything won't go perfectly as planned, but you'll give it your best shot. Don't beat yourself up.

James concluded that he really was on to something. The holes in the current assessment plan could have some unintended consequences. He needed to share that with the committee leader, Roger, and get it in front of the full committee for discussion. James thought his conclusions were obvious. Yet, given the politics involved and the direction Roger wanted to go in, he realized it would be tough to get Roger to even listen. He'd have to take it a step at a time, but he couldn't let this opportunity pass. James hoped that his reputation for integrity and commitment to the organization would give him some credibility with Roger in this early stage of their working relationship. He needed Roger to trust that he was a team player and wasn't trying to be self-serving.

Practice Vulnerability

To embrace the challenge, you have to set aside your ego and pride and be honest with yourself about the fear or discomfort you are feeling. Don't be afraid to be vulnerable. If you deny the fear and concern, you will not allow yourself to work through what is really keeping you from being courageous. Explore the cause of your fear and anxiety in facing the challenge. You want to practice informed vulnerability. You can't face your fears and work through them if you don't know what they are.

Don't be afraid to share with others that you have fears and concerns you are dealing with. (I know, this is a huge, courageous step itself.) You don't have to act like you have it all together. People can usually see through that facade. Your vulnerable moments are times when people can see you for who you are. You have no defenses up. It shows your humanity and creates a connection with others who are feeling a bit of anxiety themselves. It lets them know that being human is OK for them, too. Being vulnerable doesn't mean you're an open book. Gauge how much you share based on your relationships with different individuals.

James expected that Roger would be guarded if he approached him. Roger might see the concerns James raised as just trying to cause problems or questioning his competence as the committee leader. James didn't want Roger to feel disrespected.

Being more open about your concerns also makes it easier to reach out for help and empowers others to do the same. When a leader practices vulnerability, it sets the tone for the work environment and the type of community you are going to have. You want to create a culture of openness and trust. For example, how do you and other leaders in your organization react to employees taking risks and failing? If a leader is very critical when mistakes happen, people will be much less likely to take risks and certainly won't share information about the problems that arise. You limit the potential of the organization.

Journal about your feelings and experiences. Be attentive to times when you are feeling most fearful and vulnerable, the emotions that emerge and what the possible source may be. Also make note of what helped you to work through the challenge and the emotions. Periodically review and reflect on what you've captured to see what trends emerge and what seems to help most.

With your willingness to be vulnerable and creating an environment where perfection all the time is not the expectation, doors open to greater engagement and growth.

Reduce the Risk With Preparation

Courage materializes when you don't allow yourself to sit in fear waiting for that feeling to go away. You use fear to inspire action.

Going from being fearful and vulnerable to being courageous takes more than just building up the guts to take a step forward. Leave it up to pure guts, and fear will find its way back in. Your goal is to grow your confidence and minimize your risk so that there's little space to be fearful. You don't have control over everything, and some things are outside of your understanding. One of the most important steps to reducing risk is to prepare with a plan, anticipating what may go wrong, mitigating what you can, and putting contingency plans in place for the inevitable.

Plan Your Work and Work Your Plan

In his book *The 7 Habits of Highly Effective People*, Stephen R. Covey (1989) explains the importance of habit 2, "Begin with the end in mind," to achieving intended outcomes: "How different our lives are when we really know what is deeply important to us, and, keeping that picture in mind, we manage ourselves each day to be and to do what really matters most. If the ladder is not leaning against the right wall, every step we take just gets us to the wrong place faster. We may be very busy, we may be very efficient, but we will also be truly effective only when we begin with the end in mind."

Courage can be shattered if you miss getting to your destination because your goals and work are misaligned. You need a road map, a plan that provides guidance on how you will put courage into action.

Start with defining your hope for the outcome and outlining specific goals. How would you define success? Is the goal reasonable? What is the likelihood that the goal can be achieved? Also, consider your audience. What are their needs and expectations?

Next, direct your attention to taking steps that can help you achieve that outcome. Don't get overwhelmed with trying to plan everything at once. Focus on what the initial steps should be, and be thoughtful about the right time for taking action. What do you believe is the best path forward for all parties involved? What is the best approach to communicate your recommendations? Factor that information into your planning.

Then, run that playbook. You want to remain flexible as you receive real-time information or the situation changes.

James's apprehension was relieved as he and his colleagues laid out some action steps for how best to approach and engage Roger. They started with a clear definition of goals and outcomes. Best-case scenario would be that Roger would listen to the conclusions and recommendations and would take the lead on presenting the information to the full committee for consideration. Alternatively, a good outcome would be that, though not fully supportive, Roger would be willing to allow James to present the information and recommendations to the full committee for consideration. Worst-case scenario would be that Roger would respond defensively and decide to do nothing.

They laid out a plan for each of the scenarios. A lot was a stake for the committee, for employees, and for the organization. Knowing how to move forward and what to do in different situations, James felt more confident that they would be able to come to some agreement and work together constructively.

What-If Scenario Planning

What-if scenario planning is common in crisis management planning. By anticipating potential problems and planning how you will handle them, you have fewer unknowns, which will reduce your anxiety.

If your initial steps go as planned, what should you do next? As you make progress when you take that first step, it leads you to what the next step should be. For example, when you are driving at night, your headlights help you to see what's ahead. As you drive along, more of the road is revealed. Have a process in place to take what you have learned from your first steps to determine your next steps.

Of course, you want your plan to take you closer toward your goals. But sometimes there are things you can't anticipate, and the outcomes along your journey may not go as planned. Again, use your process to take what you have learned from your first steps to inform determining your next steps.

A Boost in Confidence and Credibility

When you are prepared, you feel more confident and come across more confident. Others can see that you are prepared and have greater confidence in you. Your outcomes are better than if you were to wing it or allowed fear to keep you from doing anything. It builds your reputation as someone who is credible.

As a talent development professional, you're often asked for your expert opinion and recommendations. You prepare your response by objectively assessing the situation to determine the best approach. Your conclusions may not agree with the solution a leader has requested, but communicating your recommendations and effectively influencing the ultimate decisions that are made will require courage. Being prepared with your assessment and a thoughtful communication plan will be important to maintaining credibility and trust.

Amy Shilliday shares her experience in handling a similar experience: "I'm not going to recommend a leader squander a lot of money and resources on training when that's not really going to solve their problem. They're going to ask me what I'm seeing that backs this up. Gone are the days when you can go into those meetings and try to sway the C-suite leadership with solely narrative. More often than not, they don't know me or my work ethic. . . . Being able to give them data to speak to what is at the root cause of the issue is very, very meaningful."

Don't Go It Alone

Humans are not self-sufficient. We have a need for human connection. Yet, there are times we feel like we can't reach out for help, especially when we are afraid, anxious, and feeling vulnerable. We feel like we have to conquer our challenges all alone or come across as being able to handle it on our own. We're too embarrassed to ask for help. However, these are the times when we need support from others the most.

Sometimes superheroes have what's called a "savior complex" or "white knight syndrome," believing they have to be the one to singlehandedly save the world's problems. Sometimes we as humans suffer from the same, feeling we have to be the fixer for everyone. Your goal is to work with others to develop innovative and effective solutions. Bringing others in also enhances ownership and support.

Though a bit embarrassed that he was nervous about addressing Roger, James pulled in his team to help him strategize and overcome his fear. He didn't let his pride keep him from inviting additional ideas and support, even reaching out to one of Roger's trusted peers, knowing he would likely need an ally to demonstrate other leaders were on board.

You need strategic allies and advocates to help demonstrate support. Those allies and advocates should be individuals with some social capital or political clout with the individuals you need to influence. Robert Cialdini refers to this concept as "social proof," one of his six principles of persuasion, which we discussed in chapter 2.

When you pull in other people, you may also be surprised to learn that your situation is not unique. Others have had similar experiences and are usually more than happy to share their lessons learned and ideas. Especially when you're in the middle of a challenging situation, it's difficult to see the situation objectively. Share what you're attempting to accomplish and what your challenges are. People have different perspectives and experiences that can help you see your situation in a different light and can be a sounding board for solutions.

You will begin to open up a support network of people who can be part of your planning and process. Trying to be courageous on your own is hard, lonely and defeating. When you reach out to the community around you, you have an abundance of resources to tap into. You have people who will stand beside you and encourage you when you feel like you "just can't." They remind you that you can, and help you succeed.

Scale Your Courage

There will be situations where you need significant courage to influence. You may not believe you can be that person of influence because you are not in a position of power. You don't have to try to become or act like a superhero. You don't have to wait for someone else to empower you. You can empower yourself. "You can start a multiplier effect simply by acting on the vision and values to which you are committed, and have a powerful impact on the organization without needing a fancy title or positional authority," encourages Catherine Perme (2016a).

Your role in talent development is fundamentally to serve others in a way that helps them exploit opportunities or to addresses problems that are preventing individuals and teams from being their best. You are not the lead actor in this movie. You play a supporting role. You influence. The individuals you are working with have got to do the work themselves. You advise, coach, encourage, and even inspire. Change will not come for them until they take the steps toward change. The courage you are building is not to make them change, but to inspire change. The courage you need is to be willing to speak up to advocate for what you believe in, to challenge the status quo, and to live according to the values you espouse.

"I definitely think that courage is part of being in talent development," says Jimmy Nelson. "Whether you're an instructor, facilitator, or instructional designer, you have to have some level of courage to say, 'This is what I believe, and I'm going to put it out there, even though people may rip it apart.'"

Without courage, you lack influence.

Summary

Being courageous is not only represented in heroic acts but is required of talent development professionals who challenge the development and growth of their organizations every day. Courage requires mental and moral strength. There are consequences to whatever decisions you make when facing a challenge, whether you take action or not. Be thoughtful and deliberate; these are mindfulness processes that will help prepare you for our next chapter discussion, being your authentic self.

CHAPTER 7

Authenticity

Tanisha understood the sensitivities around important customers, and how issues of supply chain and customer service were becoming high-profile budget concerns. Executives freely shared their opinions, ideas, and scrutiny. Both Daniel and Consuela needed their cross-functional project to go well, but how to go about managing perceptions was becoming a tough balancing act for them. In some of the senior-level meetings, Daniel would engage differently; his answers to questions were sometimes not the same as what he'd discussed with Consuela, leaving her confused. And at times, Consuela seemed to blame Daniel's team. There were other instances when they didn't know what to expect from each other and began to wonder if they could really trust each other at all.

Realizing the tension between the two, Tanisha met with Consuela and Daniel. They admitted that they were both trying to protect themselves in this politically sensitive situation and instead were destroying trust and alienating each other.

Tanisha asked them both to consider their personal values, the values of the organization, and expectations of them as leaders. As Tanisha helped Daniel and Consuela refocus on what they were collectively trying to accomplish, they outlined what they needed from each other for the working relationship to be productive. They committed to trying to be more self-aware and to taking the actions needed to ensure they worked as collaborative partners going forward. Tanisha agreed to be their conscience to help hold them accountable.

What Is Authenticity and Why Is It Important to Influence?

Have you ever encountered a chameleon and seen its color change? Chameleons have an amazing ability to change the appearance of their skin to regulate their body temperature or to reflect their mood and what they're trying to communicate. For example, when they feel relaxed, the structural arrangement of the cells beneath the skin change and reflect darker colors, such as blue. When something excites them or they feel a need to protect themselves, the cellular change reflects brighter hues of yellow, orange, and red. Chameleons also possess a long, projectile tongue used to catch their prey.

This might remind you of a few people you have encountered. People who seem to change out of the blue in ways that seem incongruent with who you thought they were and how you may normally experience them. They may unexpectedly change their opinions or behavior in a given situation and can come off as phony or self-serving. Their words and actions can sometimes be hurtful as a result, feeling like the projectile tongue of the chameleon. This type of behavior may appear advantageous; however, their perceived inauthenticity will damage their potential for genuinely personifying and being respected as a person of influence.

According to *Authenticity at Work: A Matter of Fit?* by Van den Bosch and colleagues (2019), authenticity is defined as the degree to which a person acts in agreement with one's true self. Authenticity at work refers to the extent to which we can feel in touch with our true selves while there and act in agreement within that environment.

The workplace is a dynamic environment and requires professionals to be adaptable. Different situations may call for you to be agile in shifting your behavior. But, in authenticity, that shift is consistently fundamental to who you are. That's an important distinction.

Authenticity in the workplace can be measured on three dimensions (Van den Bosch and Taris 2014). The first dimension, self-alienation, is the subjective experience of not knowing who you are at work, feeling out of touch with your true self. Secondly, authentic living reflects the degree to which you are true to yourself at work and your behaviors reflect your values and beliefs. Accepts external influence, the third dimension, refers to the degree to which you believe your behavior meets the expectations of others. "An optimal level of experience authenticity is reached when an employee experiences low levels of self-alienation, high levels of authentic living, and low levels of accepting external influence," Van den Bosch and Taris explain.

How do these dimensions show up in the persona of a leader or professional who is considered an authentic person of influence? Your behavior is guided by your personal values and principles and aligned with those of the organization. People know what to expect from you because of your consistency. You tend to be more self-aware and astutely conscientious in your interactions with others. You are confident in who you are as a person, but not arrogant, realizing that you are not perfect, and don't have to try to be. You own your mistakes and apologize for any hurt or harm that is caused. You don't try to control others' opinions or actions but are honestly interested in different perspectives. Even when a situation is sensitive or requires toughness, your motives are genuine. You do not alter the fundamental values and principles of your character based on what is required of you or who you are around. You don't take on a different personality to your advantage. You are continually striving to grow and give your best.

While we all are accountable for our behaviors, the responsibility for practicing authenticity at work is not all on the individual. Employers must create a culture where authenticity is valued, invited, and role modeled. In workplaces where this is experienced, employees report "significantly higher job satisfaction and engagement, greater happiness at work, stronger sense of community, more inspiration, and lower job stress. The more of themselves that people shared with others, the better their workplace experience," reports social psychologist Vanessa Buote (2016).

Alternatively, employee burnout, emotional exhaustion, and cynicism toward work are significant risks.

Characteristics of Authenticity

Consider Tameka. During her quarterly performance discussion, Tameka's boss, Brent, recommended she work with a coach to develop her executive presence. The recommendation came along with constructive feedback from Brent's recent observations and from one of Tameka's business partners. Tameka was concerned that being asked to work with a coach meant she had done something wrong, but Brent assured her that he believed in her potential and wanted to support her growth. Brent's feedback had always been delivered with the best intentions, and he provided space for team members to develop in their own style. He made sure he wasn't always in the limelight and was generous at giving credit to his team. Brent acknowledged his own mistakes and frustrations and would often share his own development journey in those areas. Tameka agreed to proceed with the coaching and was excited to have the opportunity.

When it comes to influence, three key characteristics are identified with authenticity: genuine motives, humility, and consistency.

Genuine Motives

When influence is most effective, your motives, or reasons for your actions, are genuine and sincere. You have a real interest in an outcome that is beneficial for all involved and, ultimately, the organization. Your goal is to not cause harm. Your motives do not just selfishly benefit your personal agenda.

"I have to be sincerely and passionately committed to the same goal and objective as the person that I'm trying to influence," says Sandi Maxey of Sandy Spring Bank. "There has to be mutual purpose and respect. Otherwise, it's just coercion and manipulation. If I'm trying to influence someone solely for the reason of self-aggrandizement, to get accolades, to get power, then that will come across. It breaks down trust. It breaks down relationships."

Humility

People want to be seen as aligning with someone who validates their own character. The expectation is that to influence, you will be a person who is worthy of trust. You will come across as competent and confident, yet humble. Much of that expectation is based on how your behaviors, decisions, and actions represent the guiding principles people associate with high levels of character. These principles, generally representing universally accepted standards of behavior within many organizations and cultures, include characteristics such as integrity, honesty, reliability, respect, trustworthiness, dependability, and humility.

Humility demonstrates that you don't attempt to influence from a place of superiority. You engage others in such a way that shows concern for their needs, respects their ideals, and creates space for them to shine.

Consistency

Authenticity is also demonstrated through your consistency. Are you consistent in your words and behavior from one interaction to another with the same person? Do you demonstrate consistency in similar situations with different people? Or, do you change your behavior based on who you are interacting with?

We look for consistency so that we know what to expect. Trust builds when you are consistent. Others can anticipate who will show up time after time when you are consistent.

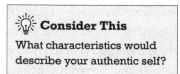

Consider This
What characteristics would describe your authentic self?

Steps to Scale Your Authenticity

The following three steps will guide you as you work to scale your authenticity:

1. Discover your authentic self.
2. Learn to be adaptable, not artificial.
3. Practice humility.

Discover Your Authentic Self

Influence requires a level of self-awareness before you even know and can interact in your authentic style. Assessments and feedback from others can be valuable information sources as you learn more about yourself.

"Authenticity begins with self-awareness: knowing who you are—your values, emotions, and competencies—and how you're perceived by others," explain professors Lisa Rosh and Lynn Offermann (2013). They also recommend reflecting on how your life and both personal and professional experiences have shaped your values, beliefs, and behaviors.

Assessments that provide insight on your personality drives, behavioral drives, communication preferences, and emotional intelligence will help provide a baseline of deeper understanding about yourself. Being in a position of influence may create some degree of stress. Assessments will help you understand your natural behavioral tendencies and how you may adapt to stressors in your environment.

Personality and behavioral style assessments provide insight into how a person is typically most comfortable approaching a situation. The early years of our lives are the most formative of our personality, which is developed around five common traits: openness to experiences, conscientiousness, extroversion, agreeableness, and neuroticism/emotional stability (Psychology Today b). Within those five traits are 32 characteristics that further define personality. Widely accepted within psychology, these traits and characteristics are reflected in a person's attitudes, beliefs, values, and behaviors. Behavioral assessments often measure how you adapt your response and reactions to external factors and situations when under stress. Reports also typically provide observations on your communication preferences and recommendations on how to more effectively communicate with others.

When you understand what motivates and drives you, you become more informed about why you do what you do. What drives you to get up and go to work every day? What drives you to contribute at the top of your game? According to TTI Success Insights (2017), "motivators can be referred to as the aspects of life that you are passionate about, things that you perceive as important, or the thoughts that provide you with purpose and direction in life." Your motivators are part of your mindset, your world-view, and, therefore, they influence your thoughts, decisions, behaviors, and actions. You are not always aware of your motivators nor are they necessarily readily apparent to others. An assessment based on the standardized categories of human motivation will reveal the combination of your primary drivers, situational drivers, and those that you are indifferent to. Be aware that what motivates you will be different from the motivators for others. Attempt to learn about what motivates others and respect these differences. Use these insights to be flexible in your interactions with others. Focusing on what is important to others will contribute to your ability to influence.

An emotional intelligence assessment will provide insight into your level of awareness of your emotions, how your emotions show up in your behaviors, and how adept you are at reading your own emotions, reading the emotions of others, and managing your own emotions to the needs of the interaction. "Emotional intelligence is the ability to sense, understand, and effectively apply the power and acumen of your emotions and the emotions of others in order to facilitate higher levels of collaboration and productivity," according to TTI Success Insights (2018).

Daniel Goleman, pioneer in emotional intelligence research and author of *Primal Leadership*, *Working With Emotional Intelligence*, and other books, lays out four domains of emotional intelligence:

- **Self-awareness.** The ability to recognize and understand your emotions and how they influence your work and interactions with others
- **Self-management.** The ability to control your emotions and behaviors
- **Social awareness.** The ability to recognize the emotions of others and read organizational social constructs
- **Relationship management.** The ability to constructively manage interactions and build relationships with others

Emotional intelligence is a developed skill and is most helpful as a person of influence. Being in tune with your own emotions and being able to manage the emotional climate in your interactions with others allows you to read and adapt to a situation more effectively. Feedback from others can also be insightful when used in combination with self-assessments. A 360-degree assessment gives you an opportunity to solicit feedback from others who work with you, including co-workers, your boss, clients you support, customers, and suppliers. This gives you insight into the experience of others in working with you.

You'll also want to check in on your stress. Sometimes stress or being in an uncomfortable position or situation can create a chameleon-like response. We can be less in control of our emotions and actions when stress arises. It's important to be aware when stress is present so that you don't become the person you don't want to be. You may use a stress assessment to reveal your level of stress and possible contributors.

From any assessments, study the results. Use the insights to inform your authentic style. What attributes most represent you? In what situations are you most comfortable? What situations bring on more stress and cause you to adapt your behavior? The recommendations in these reports will help you to enhance your communication and build better relationships. Your ability to be flexible and adapt to what others need, while being true to yourself, is a skill. It requires knowledge and action.

Going a step further, from this information, identify the characteristics that authentically reflect you. How do these characteristics align with your current reputation and with the reputation you desire? When your name comes up, what do you want people to think about you? What characteristics would you be proud for people to associate with you? Which are congruent with your personality, your values? How do these characteristics align with your professional and leadership style? How might you need to adapt your style to best align with the culture, values, and needs of the organization?

Karen was so thankful for the feedback and advice she had received from a mentor mid-career. At the beginning of their mentoring relationship, her mentor reached out to a few trusted colleagues to get a feel for Karen's reputation and opportunities for development, based on the experience others had in working with her. From these insights, Karen learned that she was very detail oriented and sometimes a perfectionist, but sometimes had a difficult time reading and adapting to the needs of others in her meetings and one-on-one interactions. Where was this coming from?

Karen's mentor suggested she talk with her boss about the feedback to see if this was a consistent theme and meet with her talent development partner to determine which assessments might be most appropriate. Karen learned that she indeed had a strong preference for details and structure. She could see it in the way she organized her office and her work. She also learned that she wasn't as aware of the emotional temperature in her interactions with others, so she failed to adapt in her approach. She was seen more as a task master. She used these insights to learn how to better sense what was going on around her and be more flexible in her work with her colleagues, while still honoring her personal needs for planning and organization.

Learn to Be Adaptable, Not Artificial

As a talent development professional, you are committed to serving others. Therefore, you must be attentive to different needs. You'll find yourself engaged in working with a variety of people and departments and addressing different needs and challenges. Your goal is to be adaptable, or flexible, in those varying situations so that you can best meet those needs, both developmentally and interpersonally.

Listen and understand the needs of others so that you can be appropriately responsive. Learn about their behavioral style and motivational drives. Adapt your interaction and communication style based on these insights. Don't get caught up in having to look good. Be willing to adapt your plans if they aren't working or aren't right for the situation.

Consistently walk the talk. The familiar saying, "say what you mean and mean what you say" could not be more relevant. Consider the characteristics you determined that genuinely represent you. Those characteristics and values to be reflected in what you say and do. Make sure your verbals and nonverbals are congruent.

Check in with yourself in real-time or in reflection to self-assess if you are being consistent. Be aware of how your colleagues approach you and how they are reacting to you. Are interactions typically more relaxed or do they seem tense and anxious? Your emotional intelligence skill can be helpful here. Identify what thoughts or emotions may be triggers to changes in your behavior. External factors such as certain situations, environments, or individuals also may be triggers to changes in your behavior.

You can influence others' behaviors, but you can't control them. The only behavior you can truly control is your own. The relationships you have with other people have a huge role in your ability to have influence and to be influenced.

There is a balance, however. Jimmy Nelson cautions to not overuse authenticity. "I have seen facilitators tell class members, 'Well, that's not how I roll. So that's not how we're going to roll in this class.' The ego coming out demonstrates that 'this class is about me, not about you.' Authenticity is important. You have to be yourself. But you also have to be the 'self' that they need."

Practice Humility

Humility is removing the focus of attention from yourself. You are modest in your opinions of yourself and how important you are. However, you do have inner confidence and portray that confidence in a humble manner. "When leaders are true to themselves and admit their mistakes or failures, it gives others permission to do the same, changing the norms of the workplace," explains Vanessa Buote (2016).

The road map to humility begins with reconnecting with your purpose. Purpose provides meaning in our lives. It helps us to discover the value we have to contribute in our work and in our lives. When we are connected to our purpose, and are working toward fulfilling that purpose, aligning our motives becomes more intuitive and the objective of our motives genuine.

As a talent development professional, your purpose is to be invested in the growth and development of the individuals and organizations you serve. Your focus, then, should be on the outcomes that realize that purpose. You genuinely want the best for others. You have a role to play in helping them achieve their best.

Why do you do this work? What does it mean for you when you have contributed to someone else's development? When your focus is on your purpose and is altruistic rather than seeking personal gain, you embody humility and can engage with authenticity.

Beware These Two Extremes

There are two extremes that affect the degree to which you can effectively embody and demonstrate authenticity. On one extreme you find yourself feeling inferior, like an imposter, and are excessively humble. The other extreme is feeling overconfident, believing you have to come across as having it all together, in control, or superior to others. Let's consider both of these extremes.

Imposter Syndrome: What to Watch Out For

"People who struggle with impostor syndrome believe that they are undeserving of their achievements and the high esteem in which they are, in fact, generally held. They feel that they aren't as competent or intelligent as others might think—and that soon enough, people will discover the truth about them" (Psychology Today nd). Such people believe that external factors such as luck, being in the right place at the right time, or being good at convincing others have helped them to achieve a position or status, but that they don't really possess the qualifications for such esteem. Maybe you recall a time in your career when you felt inferior.

At greatest risk of the imposter syndrome are women (particularly women of color, and especially Black women), and people in the LGBTQ+ community. According to psychotherapist Brian Daniel Norton, "When you experience systemic oppression or are directly or indirectly told your whole life that you are less-than or underserving of success and you begin to achieve things in a way that goes against a long-standing narrative in the mind, imposter syndrome will occur" (Nance-Nash and Norton 2020). Additionally, because corporate culture has long had disproportionately low representation of diverse groups, it is often difficult for people to see themselves as capable or that potential opportunities could be available to them.

These populations may discount their current experience or readiness for a position. Some believe they must have a higher degree of education, work experience, technical knowledge, or skills in order to be perceived qualified, as is usually the reality they experience.

There may be certain environments where the impostor syndrome is more prevalent. Within a person's family, social, and volunteer circles, the impostor syndrome may not be present, whereas at work, it may be a different story.

In their article "The Impostor Phenomenon," featured in the *International Journal of Behavioral Science,* Jaruwan Sakulku and James Alexander (2011) report that 70 percent of individuals will experience impostor syndrome at some point in their lives. "Burnout, emotional exhaustion, loss of intrinsic motivation, poor achievement, including guilt and shame about success are reinforced by repetitions of the impostor cycle."

This low self-perception will show to others a person who lacks confidence. People will not be positively influenced by you. You also will have a hard time letting your true self come through, being more protective of yourself and the perceptions other people have of you.

Impostor syndrome can be a challenge for talent development professionals. There are times you may be making recommendations to a senior-level leader on how to enhance a personal skill or facilitating technical training outside of your area of expertise. You may not feel qualified to be in an expert position in comparison to the experience and knowledge of others.

How do you overcome impostor syndrome? In my coaching work with professionals who find themselves dealing with this challenge, we begin by exploring how impostor syndrome shows up in them and what some of the contributors may be. These steps may include the following:

- Recognize and acknowledge that feeling like an impostor is sometimes a challenge for you. Self-awareness will put you in a position to work through it.
- Evaluate your expectations for yourself versus what others expect from you. Get clarity on others' expectations and negotiate reasonable terms. Let people know what you are dealing with and why you may not be able to meet certain deadlines. Align your expectations of yourself with those of others.
- Set realistic expectations with others and communicate updates. Sharing the challenges you're experiencing early on and negotiating a new deadline or deliverables will remove the stress and bring the project back to reality.
- Give yourself some grace—realize everything won't always go perfectly and there will be mistakes sometimes. Reflect on what contributed to when things didn't go as you had hoped. Leave yourself room for learning.
- Ask for help; don't go it alone. Reach out to your boss, a trusted peer, mentor, or coach. Colleagues often are very willing to help you and are just waiting to be asked. Your boss can help remove barriers for you that you don't have the political power to address. A mentor can provide feedback and be a listening ear. A coach can help you work through the syndrome.

- Focus on the value you contributed rather than your personal capability or skill. What about your personal effort contributed to the success? Ask for feedback for what others see in your work.

Superiority Complex: Could You Be at Risk?

The other extreme is believing you know more than you do or believing that you are superior to or more deserving than others. A superiority complex is a false sense of confidence without the success of achievement to back it up (Holland 2019).

For some, being perceived as superior validates their self-worth. Behaviors demonstrating superiority actually mask internal feelings or fears of inferiority, embarrassment, and disappointment. We all have shortcomings and experience what we perceive as failures. There are times when you don't want other people to know of your shortcomings. You don't want to be found out. Rather than responding in situations with honesty and working through it, you try to save face, pretending to have it all together.

There also may be a sense of entitlement, feeling like you're more deserving than others. Entitlement may come from hierarchical expectations in organizations, or from societal and cultural norms.

What are some signals that you may have a superiority complex? Following are some indicators:

- Frequent boasting
- Putting others down or minimizing the value of their ideas or contributions
- Frequently seeking validation from others
- Brushing over your mistakes, often blaming others
- Attempting to control others or a situation
- Speaking over other people or not allowing others to fully express their thoughts and ideas
- Mood swings, often feeling inferiority or anger

To overcome a superiority complex, consider these steps:

- Recognize and acknowledge that this dichotomy of experiencing inferiority but having to come across as competent is sometimes a challenge for you. Self-awareness will put you in a position to work through it.
- Be honest with yourself about your strengths and weaknesses. Ask a handful of people who you trust for their honest feedback on what they observe and what their experience is with you. Be open and not defensive in receiving what they have to share. In your interactions with other people, observe their reactions. Evaluate if the interactions are constructive or destructive. How can you help build confidence in others rather than leave them feeling less than?
- Recognize your conceit. Conceit is accompanied by arrogance. True competence and confidence are accompanied by humility.
- Manage your expectations of yourself. Don't expect that you have to be better than others or come across as perfect or superior. You're not always competing against your colleagues. Accept that you, too, have room to learn and grow. And, put your energy toward consistently delivering excellent work, not simply claiming that you do.
- Realize that you're even stronger and have greater influence when you combine forces with people who can complement your expertise. You don't have to, nor can you, know everything. As you move into leadership roles, your objective is not to be the smartest person in the room, but to have assembled the smartest people among you and be skilled at bringing out their best.
- Look for the value in others and honor them. Give respect. Earn respect in return by treating others with dignity. Have the maturity and selflessness to celebrate others' success. It's good for other people to succeed. It raises the potential of your team and your organization.

- Learn to love yourself. In our authenticity, we show our flaws and failures, acknowledge them, learn from them, and aim for improvement on the next go-round. Aspire to become the person of respected character and integrity you have the potential to be.

"I tend to be a little more forgiving and more open for those that are a little bit flawed and own up to that. I respect that. It makes people human. It makes you trust them a little more because it's not this kind of iron-clad facade that they can't do anything wrong. I can still value what they say and what they stand for," writes Amy Shilliday.

Strive for Win-Win

As you work with others and negotiate targeted outcomes, take the perspective of finding the win-win. How can both of you benefit? Will the outcome leave both better than before?

For example, you have a colleague who is always willing to help. You've helped him from time to time and feel like you can call in some favors. You are going to be attending a meeting to present the results of a recent project you led. This project and the presentation are really important for you. Leaders you want to impress are going to be in the meeting. You could use some help getting everything ready. So, you convince your colleague to help you. "This project has high visibility among the senior team. It's really important for our department to send a good impression about our work on this project and how well it's turned out. We want to set ourselves up for being able to get the funding we need for the upcoming sales enablement training."

Your colleague has been around a while and knows the players involved. It took several hours to complete the analysis and presentation slides. Your colleague reviews the details with you and helps you prepare for the presentation, ensuring you have all the background and are ready to answer leaders' questions. Going into the meeting, you feel confident. The presentation went great and you were able to demonstrate the project's successes. Impressed, leaders asked who was involved in pulling the results together. You proudly share credit with your colleague and express your gratitude for his support. Excited about the results, you rush back to celebrate with the team.

Scale Your Authenticity

Authenticity is so important for talent development professionals. Your underlying mission is to help others discover and develop their authentic best selves. "Talent development means building the knowledge, skills, and abilities of others and helping them develop and achieve their potential so that the organizations they work for can succeed and grow" (Bingham 2014). If you are so busy masking your true self, you won't know how to help others. Become better skilled at identifying what a situation calls for and responding in an authentically agile manner. What you model will empower or discourage others in their personal journey.

Whether you are facilitating a training session or coaching someone, be honest about the fact that you, too, are still a work in progress. It's easy to stand in front of the room telling participants what they should be doing, trying to come across as knowing everything in order to have credibility. Invite others to contribute their knowledge to the collective discovery and learning process.

Summary

When you are authentic, you remain true to who you are. You do not alter the fundamental values and principles of your character based on what is required of you or those around you. You are continually striving to grow and give your best. An authentic person of influence demonstrates a genuine concern for others and for achieving a mutually beneficial outcome.

Authenticity requires your skill at identifying what a situation calls for and being able to adapt within your values and the cultural norms of the organization. This work best prepares you for understanding how to use your passion, the subject of the next chapter.

CHAPTER 8

Leaning in With Passion

Twenty years Consuela had been with the company, 20 years of customer service. She was loyal to her customers, and they to the company and its many products. She was passionate about helping them and spent many days trying to do what she could to resolve inaccurate and delayed delivery issues. But her style of high-touch personal service was not sustainable.

Given Daniel's mixed messages to the C-suite, Consuela was concerned that he might not be as committed to assigning the most knowledgeable people from his team to resolving these customer delivery problems. For now, she would have to continue to be highly personally involved and dedicate resources from her own team.

But Daniel genuinely cared about their customers, too. How could Consuela assure him that she was equally passionate about taking care of customers and committed to their overall organizational success, not just that of her team? How could she show him she was deeply concerned for the success of the whole organization? By forming a project team and putting their best talent from both departments on exploring and implementing solutions, they would have the expertise and knowledge they were going to need to quickly turn this around.

Consuela began listening to Daniel. He talked about all the priorities on his plate, his concerns, and his overall objectives. She did a lot of listening. The two discussed how the customer delivery issues were affecting the business and how the lingering service issues would further impact his new supply chain processes. His team was so focused on the scale of the supply base expansion, new routing, and new logistics software implementation, he hadn't even realized the magnitude of the customer delivery issues inundating Consuela's team.

Daniel came to realize that they had the same interests at heart. He agreed that more needed to be done and that his team needed to lead the effort. Resolving these issues would take some work. He wasn't yet sure where the resources would come from given the large projects they were in the middle of. Consuela assured him that her team was on board and anxious to help. Other departments also were willing to pitch in. Consuela and Tanisha walked through the initial actions that would be necessary to get the ball rolling. Daniel and Consuela asked Tanisha to assist with identifying talent needs and, once they pulled a project team together, facilitating some team building to help them quickly begin working together. Tanisha let them both know that she was committed to partnering in any way that would add value to getting the outcome they all wanted.

Consuela was beginning to feel relieved. Finally, she thought, there was light at the end of the tunnel.

What Is Leaning in With Passion and Why Is It Important to Influence?

Leaning into your work with passion reflects a willingness to invest your time and energy into what you believe is important. Passion inspires you to strive to be and give your best. Passion sparks curiosity, a thirst for learning and growing so that you can use that knowledge to contribute in meaningful ways in your work. Your interest is in achieving the best possible outcome for and with the team. You are driven by and focused on making an impact that matters.

"Passion is an emotion that comes from within you. It is your enthusiasm, your zeal, your drive, and your motivation. You don't want to just feel passionate about your job, you want to put passion into it," writes IT manager Sam Grier (2012).

Organizations benefit from the energy and commitment passionate employees put toward achieving higher performance levels in their work. "[Passionate] workers have both personal resilience and an orientation toward learning and improvement that helps organizations develop the resilience needed to withstand and grow stronger from continuous market challenges and disruptions," according to Deloitte's report, *Passion at Work* (Hagel et al. 2014).

Passion is not a static state. An organization's culture, policies, and practices (whether formal or informal) can inspire or diminish passion. Leaders must create an environment where employees's passion is encouraged and can flourish.

When you lean in with passion, you genuinely care about the cause and the outcome. There is a purpose that drives you. You are deeply invested because of the emotional connection to a cause, a personal experience, or because you feel that your work is fulfilling purpose in your life.

Across my professional life, I have had the benefit of mentors and sponsors who invested in my development and career progression. I felt a personal responsibility and passion for reaching out to help others achieve their career goals. So, I served as a mentor and sponsor to others throughout my years working for Humana and GE. When I was laid off, that passion further turned into my life's purpose, which is the work I continue to do today. That has spurred me to invest my time, energy, and resources in sharing knowledge and developing other professionals as a coach, trainer, speaker, blogger, and author.

Earlier, education was an extremely important value. My parents enabled my siblings and me to earn college degrees to broaden our opportunities. Our mother was a Head Start teacher, passionately investing in early childhood development of toddlers across our community. She made home visits and built relationships with the families of the children in her classes. She cared deeply for them. Those values of education, service, and deep affection for others led me to be active as an operational volunteer and board member with nonprofit organizations whose mission is the educational and personal development of youth. I also serve as an instructor of up-and-coming business leaders at the college level.

Gallup's 2017 engagement research report, *State of the American Workplace*, revealed one of the 12 drivers of employee engagement: The mission or purpose of my company makes me feel my job is important. People want to feel like their lives are meaningful and look for a significant part of that fulfillment to come from their work. So, defining a purpose-driven mission for the organization and emotionally connecting employees to the mission are vitally important.

Leaders can heavily influence the emotional connection employees have with the organization's mission with clear, frequent communication, by personally demonstrating the mission and values, and working with employees to connect their work and personal passions to the mission. Genuine, meaningful purpose fuels passion and inspires yourself and others to lean in with your best effort.

In whatever situation you find yourself attempting to influence, others can tell whether what you're saying is something you truly believe. They are looking for cues that demonstrate you are credible. Why should they listen to you? Why should this be important to them? Do you believe in what you are communicating? Are you being honest?

To lean in with passion doesn't mean that you have to act like the biggest, loudest cheerleader. But, a strong belief in what you are communicating should naturally come through. You lean in to let others know you have a position, opinion, or idea that is worth their time. You make your point known. And your behavior is congruent with the message you champion. Whether you intend to or not, you are sending a message. You may say that something is important, but your body language, energy level, facial expressions, and even verbal cues will communicate otherwise. Meaningful purpose and passion elicit an energy and intention in how you engage with and influence others. What you say, how you say it, and ultimately what you do are in sync.

Characteristics of Leaning in With Passion

Let's take a deeper look at the characteristics associated with leaning in with passion: finding your passion in purpose, having the capability to contribute, and making a personal investment toward results.

Find Your Passion in Purpose

In the film *Soul*, the main character, Joe Gardner, was in search of purpose in his life. He thought that his purpose was to play with a popular jazz band. To have that opportunity would mean everything to him. But once he finally got his big chance to perform, it didn't bring him the fulfillment he expected. He was challenged to deeply consider what his true purpose was. His focus initially was on self-fulfillment. When he realized that his life's purpose and true passion was in helping others discover and fulfill their purpose, he was able to find peace.

You can only lean in with passion when you have clarity on and care about what you're leaning in about. There is a meaningful, compelling reason—a "why." And when you're trying to influence someone, you can only do so when you connect to their "why." Before someone is willing to whole-heartedly invest their time or resources, they believe there will be some emotional or tangible benefit to them, which is also often purpose driven. Deeper passion is often found within yourself when the focus is not on self, but on others.

Much like Joe Gardner's journey, your role in talent development is focused on helping others discover and achieve their full potential. Among the most rewarding sensations is the fulfillment in seeing the growth of those you work with. Many talent development professionals tell me about how sharing in these outcomes fuels their passion. A Level 3 evaluation from a time management training finds participants are getting more done during the workday by minimizing distractions. A new manager who was promoted from an individual contributor role is more confident in delegating and giving clear direction, reducing their own workload, and improving team morale. Experiencing examples like these often become your "why." You see the potential in others. You can encourage and share resources to support them in achieving that.

Gone are the days of complete command-and-control leadership, where people chose a job for a paycheck and showed up to do what they were told. In today's more engaging work environment, employees' expectations are that the workplace is more collaborative and the work worthwhile. Deloitte's research report *Leading the Social Enterprise: Reinvent With a Human Focus* (2019) describes how employees have challenged organizations to focus not only on profits, but to also elevate, hold themselves accountable to, and engage employees in fulfilling their purpose. An environment where employees can lean in with passion toward achieving a meaningful purpose has the potential to inspire commitment beyond mere compliance.

Simon Sinek explains the impact of purpose on the ability to influence in his famous 2009 TED Talk, "How Great Leaders Inspire Action." He explains that all great and inspiring leaders and organizations start with "why." "By why," Sinek states, "I mean: What's your purpose? What's your cause? What's your belief? Why does your organization exist? Why do you get out of bed in the morning? And, why should anyone care?" Their "why" defines their purpose. They are clear on their purpose and communicate to influence others based on this purpose rather than the features of their products, services, or processes. They start with the problem they solve and why it makes life better. They don't make the movement about themselves, they elevate the outcome that benefits all involved.

"People don't buy 'what' you do; they buy 'why' you do it," explains Sinek. "There are leaders and there are those who lead. Leaders hold a position of power or authority, but those who lead inspire us. Whether they're individuals or organizations, we follow those who lead, not because we have to, but because we want to. We follow those who lead, not for them, but for ourselves. And it's those who start with 'why' that have the ability to inspire those around them or find others who inspire them."

> ⌛ **Consider This**
> • What drives you to do your best work?
> • What approach do you use to tap in to the "why" of others you work with?

Have the Capability to Contribute

Beyond desire, professionals who lean in with passion have the capability to contribute in meaningful ways. That stems from applying the skills and knowledge they possess in their area of expertise. They can best contribute from their area of expertise and lean in with that focus.

They also deepen their expertise in ways that add value and add to their ongoing potential to contribute. They seek opportunities to advance their knowledge and skills so they can bring different ideas to solving challenges.

Highly passionate individuals demonstrate what the Deloitte report *Passion at Work* refers to as a commitment to domain, "a desire to have a lasting and increasing impact on a particular domain (area of expertise) and a desire to participate in that domain for the foreseeable future" (Hagel et al. 2014).

When you have a depth of knowledge in your area of specialty or industry, you can see a situation through a different lens. You can ask questions and share ideas that best fit the context of the opportunity. If you are known for your expertise, people may come to you for your opinion or advice. Your reputation as a person who is competent and who applies your knowledge with relevance and reliability has the potential to be of greater influence.

Jacqueline had 15 years of experience in learning and development evaluation and analysis within the insurance industry. In addition to being a Certified Professional in Talent Development, she had earned certificates in data and business analytics. She regularly reviewed industry and technical journals and presented on panels in industry conferences. With her technical expertise and depth of knowledge across talent development, Jacqueline was often asked to advise on the early-stage development of new programs within her company. She frequently tested new evaluation techniques and brought new ideas to the team. Her passion for her field and the contributions she could make to inspiring the growth of her colleagues was highly rewarding for her.

How you work with others also is an important contributor to your ability to add value. Your interpersonal skills are integral to being able to engage with team members in a way that resonates with their "why" and compels them to buy in.

Make a Personal Investment Toward Results

People who lean in with passion will make a personal investment of time, energy, and resources toward achieving results. They are outcome driven and eager to see results. To them, the tradeoff of the investment is worth the reward, personally and professionally. Because they feel their work and the outcome they are working toward are important, they are willing to put in the effort to achieve success.

Paula is a talent acquisition specialist with a national retail chain. Her employer was expanding locations, which meant her team would be very busy working with the stores at the local level to recruit, hire, and onboard new employees. This was an exciting time for the company, and she was eager to be a part of it. While they were working on this expansion, they would still be serving in their normal role as business partner, supporting their assigned talent acquisition needs. Paula knew how important placing the right talent would be for the success of these new locations. She had seen the impact of making the right and wrong hires in the past. With the scale of expansion and the need to get talent in place rather quickly, they would need to be innovative in their approach. The market for talent acquisition was competitive, and it would be critical to position the company well to attract ideal talent.

This type of challenge inspired Paula. She was up for the challenge. She made sure she managed her other work well to be able to devote time to explore innovative ideas. She collaborated with some of her teammates to research the latest trends in talent acquisition in other industries to see what they could apply. They reached out to people in their personal network across the markets they were expanding into to help get the word out. She and her colleagues worked closely together and hit the ground running with an infectious energy. They gained early momentum by delivering better-than-expected results in the first market. The team celebrated this early win as they expanded their focus into other markets.

When you lean in with passion, your excitement on the inside usually shows on the outside. You have an energy that makes others curious. They want to know more and, as they connect with the purpose, want to be a part of it. As they become engaged and passionate about the cause, they come into contact with other people who see their energy, growing your network of influence.

When there is a deep belief in and commitment to the "why," perseverance to accomplish the vision is stronger. That strength enables an ability to overcome the setbacks that are certain to surface. Courage is often required.

Theodore Roosevelt reminds us in his famous quote, "Nothing in the world is worth having or worth doing unless it means effort, pain, difficulty. . . . I have never in my life envied a human being who led an easy life. I have envied a great many people who led difficult lives and led them well."

The deeper the passion, the more you are determined to find a way to make it work. The setbacks and hard work required to get through them are worth it.

Steps to Scale How You Lean In With Passion

The following steps are your road map to scale how you lean in with passion:

1. Tap into "why."
2. Grow your expertise.
3. Give it your best shot.

Tap Into "Why"

It's difficult to be passionate about something if you don't know why it's important to you. Why is this (the thing you're trying to influence) something you care about? Why is it important to the organization?

Imagine you're an instructional designer and have been assigned a project to develop a training solution to enhance the personal accountability within the organization. You could approach this as if it were just another project on your to-do list, with a set of steps to follow in the design process. You'd check the tasks off on your list as you get them completed. Then, you'd be ready to turn the program over to the facilitator to prepare to deliver the training to the departments involved.

But that's not how you do things. You're known as a person who is passionate about the quality of your work and its outcomes. You realize that your contribution can make a difference to the success of the organization. You're invested in designing a solution that will help solve the challenges you understand are at stake: miscommunication, missed deadlines, and strained relationships.

How did you get to this point? First of all, you've spent time discovering what contributions you feel are personally important to make in your work—what you can offer toward achieving goals and making your workplace better. You work in talent development because you have a passion for investing in the growth and development of others. Your manager makes it a point to discuss the organization's mission, vision, and key objectives, and the role the team plays in achieving those. Additionally, she connects with each member of the team individually to discuss how their role contributes to the success of the team and to understand what is important to them personally. What you do every day is integral to the impact your team can make on the organization.

You realize that other people are depending on you with this instructional design project. Your work will be inspiring a change in behavior. If you don't take this seriously, the end product will not be effective in producing the desired results. So, you lean in to better understand the problems that are occurring and the behavior that would be most beneficial to inspiring change and helping team members work more effectively together.

You also realize that it's not enough to understand why this project is important to you. You need to understand why solving this problem is important to those directly involved. This allows you to connect the solution to their "why." Be genuinely curious about their needs, goals, and future potential. How does what you are offering help make their work or life better? How can you help them realize the outcome they're seeking? This will be your greatest opportunity to inspire change.

Connecting to your audience's "why" in your design is just the beginning. Your next challenge is to help them see and feel the connection. Compelling storytelling will enable others to connect with their "why."

As talent development professionals, our challenge is to influence others by ensuring that what we recommend is aligned with the outcomes they desire. How can you use storytelling that speaks to what is important to them, their "why," not just your "why"? Go beyond the facts and appeal to their emotions. When you understand the "why" for others, you have discovered what their emotional connection is. This is the basis around which you will make your case. Add to that your personal passion, which will help you be more authentically compelling in making connections that have the potential to influence the decisions and behavior of others.

"Influence comes down to Covey's fifth habit, seek first to understand and then to be understood," says Amy Shilliday. "And it really is about listening. When I think about influence, it's not just lobbying your ideas or what you want. It's really learning what the other person or the organization's needs and struggles are and applying a practice, behavior, or tool in a way that's going to be more meaningful for them."

Grow Your Expertise

Your capability for making meaningful contributions can scale as you acquire deeper expertise in your professional domain. You have a greater base of knowledge and experience to pull from in your work. You have greater clarity around your why because you can better contextualize your work to achievable impact and outcomes. Review the skills and experience you need to be successful in achieving the goals and outcomes of your current role. Inventory your current strengths. Do your knowledge, skills, and expertise align with your desire to lean in with passion? What skills do you need to further develop?

Sarah had chosen the field of organizational and talent development in college. Knowing how her formal education and ongoing professional development early in her career had made an impact in her life, she wanted to be able to inspire others with the same opportunities for growth. She had been working as a trainer, facilitating professional development training. She was fulfilled by seeing the behavior and career growth of her colleagues. To be able to help employees grow on a deeper level, she thought that becoming a coach would enable an ideal complement to her skillset. Sarah talked to her boss about her goals. Together they explored the coach training program and certification that would be ideal for her. She networked with her peers to get insight on their experiences and suggestions. She attended coaching-related educational programs. Several months later, she completed a coaching certification program and began to coach employees while continuing to facilitate various professional development and technical skills training programs. Sarah cared deeply for the successful growth of the people she coached and was a strong encourager of their potential. She loved her work and was excellent at it. She had trusted relationships across the organization. People often reached out to her based on the recommendations of their colleagues.

Talent development professionals are fortunate to have several avenues to grow their expertise.

Certifications help you to grow broad-based knowledge of the profession, enabling you to better understand the context and impact of your specialty. There are also certifications complementary to your work in talent development, such as in analytics or human resources.

Expertise is also acquired through your career experiences. Hands-on work experience is an excellent teacher. Consider the choices you make regarding your career path. Where do you want to be in your career in the next two moves from where you are today? What work experience, skills, and knowledge will be required to achieve that role two steps from now? What would be the next logical options to gain that experience? Do your research to get a better perspective on which roles might be most beneficial in achieving your career goals. Discuss your career goals during discussions with your manager. Work with a career coach to align your interests and your "why" with potential career options. Engage a mentor who can provide guidance on potential career options within your organization. Talk with other professionals who are in roles of interest. What was their career path? What experience, skills, and knowledge are important for success in their current role? Which roles helped them to best prepare for where they are today?

What do you want your reputation to be? What do you want to be known for? When your name is mentioned, what do people associate you with? Answers to these questions can provide some direction on where to focus your development.

Give It Your Best Shot

When something is important to you, when there is a compelling "why," you especially want it to turn out successfully. You are willing to invest your time and energy to improve the odds that things will go well. You've worked on developing your skills, and now it's time to use that knowledge and talent to do the work.

Charlie was a learning management system (LMS) administrator for a federal government agency. He was on top of the latest technologies, often appearing as a guest on podcasts and speaking at industry forums. He was recruited from private industry because of his expertise and reputation for successful LMS implementation. That was the big project waiting for him to take over when he arrived. The project had already been initiated. Being new, he would have a steep learning curve to become familiar with the organization. He would have to work with the team to quickly validate the needs previously determined for the system. He soon discovered that the current systems were outdated, and the new system implementation would provide much greater capability and allow for better management and deployment of development content for the staff. He had seen the impact in other organizations he had worked for and was anxious for his new employer to realize the benefits. The excitement was growing as others learned about the potential of what this new system could do for them. They were depending on Charlie and his team to make sure the implementation would go smoothly. He would need to readjust some of the other priorities on the team and direct some extra personal attention to ensure a successful completion.

The first thing you want to do is set a goal. What are you trying to accomplish? What are the outcomes you wish to achieve? Engage the people who are working with you in setting a target. Ensure they have clarity on where you're headed.

When passionate about achieving your goals, you are willing to get in the trenches with others to do the work. You don't just tell people what they should be doing. When you lean in, you roll up your sleeves and do your part.

For example, when you're on the board of directors of a nonprofit organization, financial grant requests are often not awarded if all the board members are not giving their time and monetary contributions to the organization themselves. Your personal giving demonstrates your belief in the mission and fiscal responsibility of the organization.

Similarly, when you're trying to influence someone, they expect that you will be "all in" with them, getting your hands dirty along with everyone else to get to the goal. Much of the work to be done will not be exciting, just as in your day-to-day job responsibilities. There will be some grunt work required, the necessary but less creative and less interactive tasks. People look at your willingness to do some of the less glamorous work that needs to be done as an indication of your commitment.

If you are facilitating a training session on how to improve communication by listening, yet participants experience you constantly butting in to finish their sentences or easily getting distracted when someone is talking with you, that demonstrates that you haven't been willing to work on improving your own listening skills. So, why should they?

Much of the work in organizations is done in teams. And, to give it your best shot, you will need the support of your team and others in your organization. Be thoughtful about how you will engage others in the work. You may sometimes play more of a supporting role, coaching and encouraging others along the journey. Be sure that there is clarity about roles, responsibilities, and expectations of those involved.

Sometimes in our attempts to influence the decisions and behaviors of others, we share the "why" and the "what" but forget to provide the "how." These days, you'd hardly dare travel anywhere unfamiliar without a GPS to provide step-by-step instructions for your route. Missing a turn could take you way off course and cause you to lose precious time. Your GPS gives you a good line of sight to the miles to be traveled, the route you need to take, the length of time it will take. This allows you to better plan for your trip. It even warns you when road construction or a traffic accident will require you to take a detour. Teams need this guidance, too.

You've gotten buy-in and generated energy by making that emotional connection. People are on-board and ready. But they don't necessarily know how to get to started or what to do next. The plan is not well communicated.

One of the common reasons that projects fail is team members don't have the tools and techniques they need to produce consistently successful projects, according to authors Richard Discenza and James B. Forman in their 2007 Project Management Institute conference paper, "Seven Causes of Project Failure." This issue extends across all different applications in the workplace.

People need a road map that provides guidance for how to achieve the goal the team is setting out to accomplish. Engage them in developing the plan, connecting to their "why" through the process. Ensure the required resources will be available and that people are clear on roles, responsibilities, and expectations. People need to know what will be required of them, what resources they will need, how much time it will take, and what they can expect along the way. Define a path for others to come alongside you so that collectively, you give it your best shot.

Leaders need to be willing to do the work, according to James Kouzes and Barry Posner. They discuss these conclusions in their book *The Leadership Challenge* (1995), as part of one of the Five Practices of Exemplary Leaders, Model the Way: "When leaders ask others to change, it's not enough to simply deliver a rousing speech. While compelling words may be essential to lifting people's spirits, leaders know that constituents are more deeply moved by deeds. Constituents expect leaders to show up, to pay attention, and to participate directly in the process of getting extraordinary things done."

Be willing to lead the way and give it your best shot.

Scale How You Lean in With Passion

The next time you're attempting to influence a leader on your training recommendations, a talent needs assessment, or talent acquisition plan, or are working to influence behavior change among participants in a training program, lean in with passion.

Get clear on your "why" behind your recommendations and communicate that. Demonstrate your passion and commitment. Identify what's important to whom you're communicating with and connect with them emotionally by using compelling storytelling about how your recommendations help them achieve their own "why." Grow your skills and expertise so that your time and energy invested are effective in moving the ball toward the goal line.

Summary

While a strong purpose or "why" fuels passion toward your work, you can challenge yourself further to learn and grow by helping others achieve their "why." The combination of commitment, recognized expertise, and achievement elevates your influence potential, extending your engagement and reach, pointing us toward the subject of chapter 9.

CHAPTER 9

Engaging a Diverse and Inclusive Workplace Community

The project slated to improve customer on-time delivery and order accuracy was finally launching. Things needed to move quickly. Frustrated customers were not yet feeling the organization-wide changes Consuela and Daniel envisioned. The two had created a formal project charter and began to work with Tanisha on talent acquisition and development plans. They reviewed the data analyses again to determine the functional expertise and skill sets needed. This team would be diverse. The project would need employees from other departments besides Consuela's customer service team and Daniel's supply chain team. They would need to pull from product management, manufacturing, finance, quality and service, and would need to involve a few employees from different shifts. They would also need to partner with talent development, as process updates would require revamped training.

Many of these departments had their "go-to" employees whom they would often tap for different projects. But Tanisha wanted to ensure that the selection for this team included those who usually did not get such an opportunity to participate in high-profile, business-critical projects. There were outstanding, often diverse, talent who were often overlooked and underutilized. These employees needed the experience and exposure to showcase what they were capable of contributing to the organization.

Once the project team staffing was completed, Tanisha worked with the project leader from Daniel's team, Bret, to plan an initial kickoff meeting and team-building session. Several of these employees had not worked together before. The company also had an issue with departments working in silos. So, getting team members to trust each other, share information and resources, and support each other would take some work. Tanisha agreed to coach Bret throughout the project to ensure he could effectively work through these issues with the team.

As people arrived for the kickoff meeting, Tanisha welcomed each member of this diverse group, noting to herself the intersection of expertise and characteristics that made these individuals unique. She, Daniel, and Consuela were excited to see what this team would be able to accomplish.

As part of the engagement and community-building process, Bret met with each team member individually to get to know them personally and professionally, their interest in being on the team, their skills, and how they thought they may be able to add value. He shared why the project was so important to the organization and ways he thought they could be involved. He also made space for the diversity of opinions and ideas to surface. During the team building, they discussed expectations of each other, considered the intersectional diversity each person brought to the table, and decided how they would respect and honor each other and their differences in perspective. They had to establish some new team norms for how they would work more closely together as a community, though their departments were not necessarily used to working together in the same manner.

The community that was created with this project team influenced the support they were able to get from other departments when needed. The diversity of this team was one of the greatest assets for what they were able to accomplish.

What Does It Mean to Engage a Diverse Workplace Community, and Why Is It Important to Influence?

What does it mean to engage a diverse and inclusive workplace community and why is it important to influence? You can probably list several groups you're in—a professional association, your alma mater alumni group, or even the team you're on at work. The gathering together of people with a common interest may create a group, but that group is not necessarily a community.

What makes a group a community?

In their book, *Creating Community Anywhere: Finding Support and Connection in a Fragmented World*, authors Carolyn Shaffer and Kristin Anundsen (1993) describe the behavior of a community: "Community is a dynamic whole that emerges when a group of people:

- Participate in common practices.
- Depend upon one another.
- Make decisions together.
- Identify themselves as part of something larger than the sum of their individual relationships.
- Commit themselves for the long term to their own, one another's, and the group's wellbeing."

There is an alignment around a purpose that adds meaning for the community. The community engages in what author and editor Ron Zemke (1996) called "mutual striving" to achieve a meaningful, worthwhile goal. Purpose alignment, mutuality, and collaboration do not mean that a community is void of conflict, but because of those, they are able to work through discord when it occurs.

Feeling a sense of community goes beyond the physical presence of being together or striving together. A significant part of the experience of community is also a psychological one. "The psychological sense of community at work refers to a worker's sense of membership, participation, and identification with some work or work-related group" (Klein and D'Aunno 1986). There is a sense of "we're in this together," which establishes a commitment to the outcome and, for each member, a responsibility to play their part.

Now, consider the communities you are a member of. How would you describe your experience with those communities to which you favorably feel a part? Do you share a common interest, a common passion? Are you working toward a worthwhile goal? Do you have opportunities to contribute, using your skills and bringing your ideas and thoughts from your unique experiences? Do you feel a sense of mutual respect within the community? Do members hold the best interest for the group and each other? Do members look out for each other? Are they willing to lend a helping hand?

While community implies "togetherness," it takes intentional effort to develop inclusion within that togetherness. Inclusion fosters community. Norms of inclusive communities involve reaching out to invite, extend membership to, and welcome others who are diverse, recognizing the diversity of the community as a strength.

Why do we care about building a diverse and inclusive community rather than simply being satisfied with coexisting as a collection of workplace groups?

"A sense of community invigorates members' lives with a sense of purpose and a feeling of belonging to an integrated group that is doing something worthwhile," explains Gilbert Fairholm in *Perspectives on Leadership: From the Science of Management to Its Spiritual Heart* (1998). Building community forms healthy working relationships, and those relationships create stronger emotional connections that can lead to greater workplace belonging and commitment. Further outcomes of a sense of community may include a more positive self-concept, enhanced self-respect, improved morale, and a perceived security about their place in the community, all of which can help to reduce stress and enhance work performance.

A study on workplace belonging by BetterUp Labs (2019) found that employees with a strong sense of belonging had higher productivity and overall work performance, lower turnover, and lower rates of absenteeism, and their employers benefited with improved financial performance and productivity. Fundamental to being a person of influence in the workplace is meeting performance expectations and contributing to the goals of your team and organization.

Building a diverse and inclusive community fosters greater value among members and stronger relationships and social capital with each other. From the trust that is present, influence among members of the community can result. Community members are more empowered, they have a voice, and each plays an integral role. They come together as a cohesive unit, demonstrating collective support for their purpose and goals, which can enhance overall influence outside the community.

If we as humans are in a sea of sameness—little diversity of thoughts, ideas, perspectives, talents and skills, and experiences—we end up with more of the same, over and over again, and little growth. This is not an uncommon condition in organizations. To move beyond this state to one of community, diversity, equity, and inclusion is important.

Jackson was the director of organizational development for a telecommunications company. Historically, the different departments across the company worked in silos, making it difficult to get things done, especially if you needed a decision or action quickly. Jackson was determined to change the culture and knew one of the best ways to do that was to lead by example. He had attended a session on building diverse and inclusive communities in the workplace at a professional conference and had gotten some ideas about where to start. Not being embarrassed to turn the mirror on himself, he discovered there was opportunity for his own team to work better together. While the team set collective goals each year, there wasn't clarity and engagement around the real purpose of the team and the ultimate outcomes they were working toward. Therefore, despite the agreed-upon department goals, people still had disparate goals and agendas.

Jackson recognized that the composition of his team primarily consisted of people with the same professional background and experience. Those with different credentials were not valued the same. And, though he had worked to recruit demographically diverse people on his team, all were not equally empowered. Externally, other department leaders and employees did not see the organizational development team as strategic partners. They were invited to meetings when someone had a specific request but weren't there to influence strategic decisions. Their influence as a department, and as individuals, was not as great as it could be, and frankly needed to be. They called themselves a team, but, upon exploring further, Jackson learned that people were not feeling a genuine sense of value, belonging, or community.

Your work environment may be diverse, but inclusion may not be ingrained in the culture. Inclusion manifests in how the organization's values are carried out in company policies and procedures, career opportunities, how people interact with each other, and the intention with which all employees are a part of the fabric of carrying out the organization's purpose.

Influence is most effective when it is shared and extended. If you feel like someone is communicating with you based on a level of respect for who you are, you are more open to their influence. Consequently, with mutual respect, influence is extended as an openness in communication and flow of ideas take place.

As work within organizations is shifting to more cross-functional, project-based teams, the ability for diverse teams to work inclusively in community is essential.

"If you are in a leadership role, you really need to be attentive to how you can build community and contribute to the success of all members of your team," says training and development expert Amy Shilliday. "You have significant influence. Part of your influence is just being 100 percent there to support each person through whatever they're going through. You are in an ideal position to extend influence to your team by empowering them in their roles and showcasing their talents."

Characteristics of Engaged, Diverse, and Inclusive Workplace Communities

What characteristics are representative of engaged, diverse, and inclusive workplace communities? These communities possess a deep commitment to a shared meaningful purpose, they value and practice inclusion, and within them empowerment is extended across the community.

Deep Commitment to a Shared, Meaningful Purpose

"Perhaps the single most important element in a real community is the commitment by its members to a shared vision of the future" (Naylor, Willimon, and Osterberg 1996).

The formation of a group doesn't make it a community. There is an evolution that takes place as groups work toward community. Communities form around a shared purpose, as do groups. You are part of various groups at work that share a common purpose or goal. You can work with a group to achieve that goal, but to what degree are the members of the group committed to the outcome, the vision of the future state? As people come into the group and are introduced to the purpose, they test the purpose against their own personal values and priorities. Is there a mutual benefit for all members, or will the advantage skew to some members of the group? Observe whether there is alignment around—and unselfish commitment to—the vision among other members of the group. Deep commitment inspires accountability among members to do their part to successfully achieve the goal.

A community's strength is generated by inviting and welcoming all the assets that come from people's uniqueness. Because of your relationships, you integrate compelling storytelling that makes a personal connection with others. You make a strong case by tapping into what's important to the community. The community grows its influence by inspiring members to tell their stories to engage others.

Value and Practice Inclusion

Leaders often mistakenly believe that the singular goal of DEI initiatives is to ensure their teams and organizations are diverse, comprising employees who represent commonly thought-of differences, such as race, gender, ethnicity, or sexual orientation. If they have more employees who are representative of these basic areas, they also consider themselves to be inclusive, as they are including more of these diverse employees in their organization. This is a misunderstanding.

"Diversity is about the mix of individual differences (such as race, gender, beliefs, age, skills, experiences, and so forth) across an organization; inclusion is about ensuring that the mix of individuals and their differences are valued and respected. While you need D&I in your organization, they are separate entities and have different focuses for developing them," explains Joy Papini (2020).

Every person is diverse in some way, possessing characteristics that make them uniquely who they are. Inclusive communities work intentionally to engage members, inviting and valuing the diversity that each individual brings. When groups or organizations are not inviting and welcoming of diversity, in-groups and out-groups form, intentionally or not. The in-groups, whose members represent sameness and are only open to membership of certain people, come across as having an attitude of superiority over others. People not in the in-groups feel a greater sense of exclusion and isolation. "Exclusivity is considered an enemy of community, because it can turn the potential community into nothing more than a clique, a group organized to protect against a feeling of community," caution Jo Manion and Kathleen Bartholomew in "Community in the Workplace: A Proven Retention Strategy" (2004).

"People who acknowledge that others' needs, values, and opinions matter to them are often the most influential group members, while those who always push to influence, try to dominate others, and ignore the wishes and opinions of others are often the least powerful members," write community psychologists David McMillan and David Chavis in "Sense of Community: A Definition and Theory" (1986).

Empowerment Is Extended
With a passion and emotional connection to the "why," people within the community are actively engaged in fulfilling the purpose. They are

committed to success and offer their talents, ideas, and resources to enable success. They have a sense of belonging, which is reinforced in how they are treated with respect and appreciated for their contributions.

Members are not only enlisted in the purpose of the group, they are also invested in its relationships. Because the focus and commitment of each member is directed toward the fulfillment of the purpose, there are fewer concerns about personal agendas. Inclusion fosters greater trust and psychological safety. As members collaborate and offer support, social capital within relationships deepens. Members feel a greater sense of ownership and are empowered with a voice in the decision making and direction of the community.

People are not passively, but actively engaged, willingly utilizing the value and talents they have to contribute. They have a place to contribute that is welcoming of their value. They are invited to be part of the community, involved in giving their input and making decisions. The environment is one where information is shared and communication transparent. "Workplace community will not flourish if it is dominated by a handful of people possessing a disproportionate amount of power and influence" (Naylor, Willimon, and Osterberg 1996).

"Another part of influence is inviting people to share what is on their mind," reflects Sandi Maxey. "I'm interested in what you have to say. And I'm willing to change my mind based on what you have to say. This is a collective effort."

Steps to Scale Engaging a Diverse and Inclusive Workplace Community

The following steps are your road map for engaging a diverse and inclusive workplace community:

1. Cultivate diversity and inclusion.
2. Inspire belonging and engagement.
3. Unleash community influence.

Cultivate Diversity and Inclusion

Diversity and inclusion initiatives must have active executive-level sponsorship and support and be a strategic leadership priority to have a chance at changing the overall organizational culture. If those types of decisions are not in your control, what can you do?

Whether your organization has made diversity and inclusion a priority or not, that doesn't prevent you from individually making it a personal value that you act upon. Whatever your role in the organization, diversity and inclusion can be a priority in your own work, even if it is not an official initiative within your organization. You can influence and make a difference for the people in the communities you are a part of.

Your intention has to be both creating a diverse community and being inclusive of the diversity within the community. To be open to understanding and embracing diverse individuals in an inclusive manner, we need a good sense of compassion. Nate Regier (2019), an expert in compassionate accountability, says, "Compassion is an action verb originating from the Latin root meaning 'to struggle with.' Compassion says, 'We are in this together.'"

Regier explains that for compassion to work, three switches must be turned on in your mindset:

- **Value.** You see value in yourself and others, and champion equality.
- **Capability.** You see yourself and others as capable of contributing, leverage the diversity, and invest energy in further growth and development.
- **Responsibility.** You take ownership of your feelings, thoughts, and behaviors and allow others to do the same. You own your part in creating a better tomorrow.

These three mindset switches are essential elements in the work of talent development. In order to feel worthy of having something to contribute to the development of others and be confident in yourself, you need to value yourself, believe you are capable, and take responsibility for applying appropriate methodologies for creating optimal development experiences. To see value and capability in others, encourage their personal responsibility in the development process; this offers the best opportunity for them and your learning solutions.

One of the areas talent development is rapidly shifting is in how job descriptions are written to be more inclusive. In the article "How Changing One Word in Job Descriptions Can Lead to More Diverse Candidates," Courtney Seiter (2015) discusses how social media tech company Buffer went about shifting the terminology in their job descriptions, helping them to attract a more diverse candidate pool. Previously, less than 2 percent of their candidate pool was women. They moved away from the term "hacker" as a job title, for example, and replaced it with "developer," being more reflective of the role, and included more of what it's like to work for the company in the job description.

Shift the lens through which you see and perceive yourself and other people. Remove the bias and judgment in your policies and practices. Commit to doing your part to making inclusion a reality.

"Talent development professionals specifically really need to take a deep dive into their own belief system, values, and perspectives," says talent development leader Jimmy Nelson. "If there are parts in the back of their brain that keep them from including a group or appreciating the value that someone brings, that's an opportunity for personal development."

Inspire Belonging and Engagement

Building community begins with shared commitment among members to its purpose and future vision. People are looking to see if your community is really inclusive, having any real knowledge or concern for what is important for them. Are there people involved who look like me? Are there people involved who share my interests and aspirations?

Assist others in identifying where they fit within the community. You need to understand more about their "why," where they connect emotionally, and communicate the "why" and goals of the group in a way that is compelling for them. People will also need to determine if there are common values they share with the community. "Cooperation, trust, and human empathy are among the shared values which are vital to the formation and survival of communities," Naylor, Willimon, and Osterberg (1996) describe in their article "The Search for Community in the Workplace."

Once a person determines they identify with the purpose and values of the community and have a place in achieving its fulfillment, how do you go about engaging them in the community? Communities are formed around the relationships people have with each other. The social capital within the community that builds from valuing and practicing inclusion strengthens belonging and engagement.

Reach out to expand your community, inclusively connecting with others who are not just like you. If you don't have an intention about reaching out to others outside of what you closely identify with, then you won't. Do you intentionally go out to lunch with different people? Are you inclusive in recommending talent for development and career advancement opportunities? Reaching out to connect with people you initially know nothing about is uncomfortable. You are most comfortable with the people who are most familiar to you, having many of the same characteristics that you do. Here is where vulnerability comes into play again. People are often threatened by others who are different from them because they don't know them. They make assumptions about them based on conscious stereotypes they believe or the unconscious biases they may carry from their life experiences. People may ask, "Well, what do I say? What will we talk about?"

Start by exploring the dimensions of diversity you identify with yourself. A tool such as the Diversity Wheel created by diversity, equity and inclusion expert Marilyn Loden, or the Table of Diversity developed by diversity, equity and inclusion expert Demetria Miles-McDonald, will help you discover the characteristics that best represent you. These tools include characteristics such as the common diversity elements of race, ethnicity, age, gender, sexual orientation, and physical abilities, as well as characteristics not as commonly thought of with the word "diversity" such as military status, education level, political beliefs, geographic location, job type, and family status.

Identify the top five dimensions that relate the most to how you see yourself. Why these five? What privileges have these dimensions afforded you in your life? What barriers have been present for you as a result of these dimensions of your identity? How has that impacted your self-perception? How others see you? What related life experiences stand out for you?

Then consider the diversity dimensions that least represent you. What groups are representative of the dimensions you are least familiar or comfortable with? These can be a starting point for where you make intentional connections with others.

Do your homework to better understand individuals in these groups. You may use contacts within your network to make connections. Use various contextual resources to research information that will help you to be more informed. Be careful about extending generalities or stereotyping any individual based on what you've learned. Make it a point to get to know people on an individual level within your own department, with participants in your training workshops, and with people on the front lines in your organization. You may discount the value and capability of some of these individuals simply because you don't know them. Explore what you have in common as a starting point in building community.

Building workplace communities that are diverse and inclusive begins with expanding your circle to be inclusive of the different cultures, opinions, experiences, and expertise that contribute to a vibrant community. You invite engagement and convergence by growing an understanding and respect for each person. You are proactive at enhancing your knowledge about the members of your community. You build social capital by adding value in the relationship.

Curiosity is key to getting to that level of insight. Amy Shilliday shares how being curious has helped her to connect and build greater trust: "If we're always curious and approach everything with that curious mindset instead of being judgmental—how does this work; tell me more about this; why is this set up this way—we can have greater influence. It goes back to that trust factor. People feel more comfortable giving you information when they don't feel like you're attacking or judging them."

☼ Consider This

- Explore the dimensions of diversity you personally identify with by reflecting on the following questions. Refer to tools such as the Diversity Wheel and the Table of Diversity noted in this chapter as a resource.
- Identify the top five dimensions that relate the most to how you see yourself. Why these five?
- What privileges have these dimensions afforded you in your life? What barriers have been present for you as a result of these dimensions of your identity?
- How has that impacted your self-perception? How others see you? What related life experiences stand out for you?

Unleash Community Influence

The power of a workplace community is in the commitment and willing involvement of its members, inspiration derived from the community's purpose, an ownership to fulfilling its mission, and genuine respect and care members have for each other. Because of that connection, members need to be actively and purposefully involved if a community will have a chance of being sustained.

Author and management professor Henry Mintzberg (2009) suggests that community leaders shift from leading from the top down to leading from the center, reaching out to form more of what he calls "communityship." "A community leader is personally engaged in order to engage others, so that anyone and everyone can exercise initiative," he explains. The leader is not calling all the shots. Influence is distributed among the members of the community. A leader or any member of the group does not have to grant empowerment to members but can cultivate an environment where influence can be unleashed.

Diversity and inclusion play a role in creating this type of environment. While members of a community may have a voice, do they feel comfortable using their voice on behalf of the community, and are they trusted to do so? Sometimes people are just waiting to be asked. They may be intimidated by others who seem to be more in the in-group, and don't really know yet if they have a place within the community.

During his training programs, Leon works to create a learning community among participants, which starts before they show up for the program on the first day and continues after the formal program sessions conclude. He facilitates introductions beforehand and helps participants realize how they play a crucial role in the learning experience and influence the outcomes for each member of their community. He invites contributions to decisions about the learning process so that each member is invested in the learning outcomes. He makes sure everyone has a chance to share their perspectives and ideas as a way to facilitate greater learning, inviting and respecting the uniqueness each person offers. His philosophy is that everyone has something to offer. Often, a person may not have had the opportunity for that "something" to be discovered within themselves. They may have been invisible based on societal and organizational biases, policies, and practices, and therefore, not afforded the same opportunities as others to develop themselves, to speak up or to contribute. He is determined to change that. These learning communities were nurturing new relationships and inspiring a broader community of professionals of influence across the organization.

Tap into the power of the variety of skills, experiences, and ideas people bring. When you are investigating a new learning management system or identifying needs for a new course, you may have overlooked frontline or junior-level employees as potential subject matter experts. When asking for input during a training workshop, invite divergent opinions to be able to explore all sides of an issue more objectively and creatively. Don't be threatened because of the talents someone else has to offer. See their contributions as a collective strength that, when pooled together, enhance your capacity to achieve your goals. Talk with others about their skills and interests. Make suggestions about what a good fit might be.

To make better decisions and achieve the most effective business outcomes, you need the voluntary effort of team members to give their best. "Leaders can't survive on their own, nor do they have all the answers," Gallup's 2017 *State of the American Workplace* study notes. "Asking for and considering individuals' input leads to more informed decision making and better results. This element of engagement is powerful and measures employees' sense of value and inclusion. Employees who believe they are heard feel appreciated for their insights and have opportunities to make significant contributions to their work environment."

Scale Your Engagement of a Diverse and Inclusive Workplace Community

Engaging diverse and inclusive workplace communities is integral to the mission and strategic initiatives of talent development. Your role is to help unleash talent potential and, ultimately, organizational potential. Work with key stakeholders to make diversity and inclusion foundational to organization development, integrated across stages of the employee life cycle: selection, onboarding, skills development, performance management, career development, and succession. The work of talent development will be more effective if you have a more diverse and inclusive community working with you, championing, supporting, and included in your initiatives.

"When it comes to the talent development industry, we should be helping to drive diversity and inclusion, not just taking a back seat as participants in the training sessions. People who are not inclusive, especially for what we do, will not be successful long-term. Guaranteed," says talent development leader Jimmy Nelson.

A workplace community that fosters inclusion and belonging has the capability to expand influence from a select few to many. In an environment where you experience community within your direct work group or department and with the partners you support, trusted relationships and partnerships strengthen. This creates conditions for you to be a person of influence within the community, and for the community to be a collective influence outside of itself.

Summary

Diverse and inclusive workplace communities foster a greater sense of belonging and result in higher levels of overall employee performance. As community members commit to a greater purpose and build social capital, influence expands because of the relationships of trust, respect, and common experience. The community's influence extends beyond its members, reaching out to engage others. This may seem a long way from where we began at the outset of this book considering how one individual could become a person of influence. In the next chapter, I'll describe how you can put it all together by scaling your influence.

CHAPTER 10
SCALE Your Influence

Tanisha sat down with a sigh of relief, reflecting on where they had started and how far they had come. If she had not been able to persuade Consuela to reconsider how to use her influence, they might be looking at a very different situation right now. Consuela would have had a much tougher time getting Daniel to realize she wasn't blaming him or pushing more work on him but was invested as a partner. Consuela was growing a lot through the process and was earning greater respect and trust among her peers and senior leaders. She grew the social capital with her team. She was honest early on about her skepticism regarding getting support outside of customer service to resolve the issues. She had the courage to go to bat for her team, as tough as it was, and they never forgot that.

Tanisha could see a change in Daniel as well. This project put him in a politically sensitive position. As he realized Consuela and Tanisha had his back and were in this challenge with him, he let down his defenses, sometimes demonstrating courage in pushing back and speaking up for what he believed was the right thing to do.

Tanisha had been surprised how Consuela and Daniel had responded to this challenge. She'd known Consuela for her hard-driving, go-it-alone work ethic, but this experience had forced her to reach out to others in ways that must have been uncomfortable for her. She'd always been confident, verging on brittle; now there was an expansiveness in her demeanor; she seemed more relaxed and secure. Daniel, on the other hand, was a bit of an enigma. He also had become more public, now a regular presence on the agenda of senior-level meetings he never had to deal with before, but he could be a subdued presence as he tried to navigate the expectations of his new responsibilities. Whenever he met Tanisha for coffee, though, he was the same old affable Daniel. As her own team had grown in size and responsibility, Tanisha realized how her own influence had grown, and she didn't take it lightly.

A Privilege and Responsibility

Influence is earned. To influence is a privilege. To be a person of influence is a responsibility.

There is power in influence. How you use it calls you to be accountable. Your influence can help or hurt, inspire or incite, empower or destruct. Your influence has consequences on other people's lives and livelihood, as well as your own. Your influence should have a conscience.

Never forget that influence is more about how you live than what you do. Influence goes beyond the tactic you choose to use to convince someone. The values and motivations that drive how you live manifest in your words, behavior, and choices in how you influence. Your words, behavior, and choices leave a mark in this world. As inconsequential as they may seem, the consequences (intended or unintended) are real. How will your conscience show up based on the decisions you make? If you are a person of integrity and intention, your soul tells you whether you're doing the right thing, influencing honorably, or not. Do you listen?

I encourage you to take your responsibility seriously and influence for good. Live the person of influence you are becoming.

Becoming a Person of Influence

"As long as you're growing and developing and moving in the direction that makes you a better person, overall then I think your influence will grow," Jimmy Nelson says. "If you ever stop and think, 'I'm done.' 'I've got this.' 'I'm good.' . . . that's when you fall down. A lesson I learned about influence is that you have to be continually changing, continually adapting yourself, modifying your perspectives, and looking at yourself in a deep way."

Our work in talent development spans across the organization to ensure talent is prepared and enabled to meet mission outcomes and performance goals now and in the future. It is not enough to solely focus on meeting today's needs. Talent development professionals are forward thinkers and innovators. We are change agents. To do that effectively requires us to courageously challenge ourselves and our organizations to grow.

Organization design is moving more toward cross-functional teams than the traditional silos we're used to operating in. Where work is performed is changing, with more remote or hybrid work arrangements continuing into the unforeseeable future. The evolution of the knowledge and technological economies our organizations compete in is more rapid and dynamic than ever. This requires retooling organizations and reskilling our human capital. Talent development is at the forefront in all of this, influencing how our organizations, and the talent within them, are able to not only adapt, but also lead the way into the future. Whatever your talent development role, you influence these outcomes.

What does that mean for you? How do you become that person of influence you personally aspire to, and for developing the influence culture within your organization?

Your road map focuses on two key areas:

1. Engage the influence with SCALE principles.
2. Develop the competencies identified for success in your profession.

Engage the Influence With SCALE Principles

Influence is a critical soft skill for any leader or professional. If you have positional power, you may believe that influence automatically comes with your positional status. You are sadly mistaken. Your referent power may earn you compliance among those you lead. It takes work to gain their emotional commitment.

Influence, like true leadership, is earned. The influence principles outlined in this book will enable you to scale your practice to a deeper level of influence with peers, your manager, leaders, direct reports, partners, and customers.

Assess Your Competency Across the Influence With SCALE Principles

Self-awareness is a critical starting point. In the resources section of this book, you will find a self-assessment to rate your current practice on each of the five influence with SCALE principles. Complete the rating exercise. Then, record your rating (circle) for each of the five principles in Table 10-1.

Table 10-1. SCALE Principle Rating Exercise

How would I rate my current practice?

	I really need to work on this principle			I'm doing very well in this principle	
Social capital	1	2	3	4	5
Courage	1	2	3	4	5
Authenticity	1	2	3	4	5
Leaning in with passion	1	2	3	4	5
Engaging a diverse and inclusive workplace community	1	2	3	4	5

Identify a Starting Point and Take Action

Your next step will be to identify a starting point to further develop your influence practice. These principles are not linear and don't need to be developed that way.

Principles rated 4 or 5 are areas where you're already doing well. What specific practices from these principles should you continue? Focus on being intentional about your actions on these areas of strength first. These will benefit you the most. Refer back to the characteristics of these principles in each chapter. How can your practice in these principles replicate these outcomes?

Which areas may need more attention? Principles rated 1, 2, or 3 are areas you feel you need to work on and will be your focus for further development. Begin with the principles you rated 3. You can more easily move these principles to a 4 or 5. Ask yourself the following questions:

- If more than one principle is rated a 3:
  - Given your current role, the current work environment you're in, or present situation, which principle do you believe would be most beneficial to focus on first?
- What stood out to you when you reflected on why you gave yourself this rating?
- Refer back to the characteristics of these principles in each chapter. How can your practice in these principles replicate these outcomes? What would you like to see happen?
- What steps should you take to better scale your influence in this principle?
  - What one step can you take in the next seven days that will benefit you most?

The action steps for each principle are noted here for your reference:

Steps to Scale Your Social Capital

1. Reach out.
2. Selflessly add value.
3. Build respect and trust.

Steps to Scale Your Courage

1. Embrace the challenge.
2. Reduce the risk with preparation.
3. Don't go it alone.

Steps to Scale Your Authenticity

1. Discover your authentic self.
2. Learn to be adaptable, not artificial.
3. Practice humility.

Steps to Scale How You Lean in With Passion
1. Tap into "why."
2. Grow your expertise.
3. Give it your best shot.

Steps to Scale How You Engage a Diverse and Inclusive Workplace Community
1. Cultivate diversity and inclusion.
2. Inspire belonging and engagement.
3. Unleash community influence.

Commit to taking action. Use the job aids, tools and resources found in the resources section of this book to help you begin taking steps toward an accelerated transformation. (Resources are also downloadable at InfluenceWithScale.com.) Share your goals with someone who will help keep you accountable and on track. Review your progress along the way. Pat yourself on the back for having the courage to move forward and for what you're able to accomplish.

Develop the Competencies Identified for Success in Your Profession

If you want to be a person of influence, you must have a good foundation in the competencies identified for success in your profession. Your ability to track and record how you contribute to business results builds a base level of credibility. For talent development professionals, you could work toward proficiency in the three domains of ATD's Talent Development Capability Model. Whether you are a talent development professional or not, and especially if you are a leader, you are expected to effectively apply essential soft skills (Personal Capability), demonstrate sound technical expertise and leadership skills (Professional Capability), and make a meaningful impact on achieving organizational objectives and growing talent capability (Organizational Capability). You can't be a person of influence without this substantive foundation. And you must effectively demonstrate that you possess these capabilities. You are able to scale your influence when this foundation is evident. This is not a one-and-done process. Your development and demonstration of these competencies is ongoing.

If you are not a talent development professional, determine the competencies that are applicable for your area of expertise or industry. The basic framework of personal, professional, and organizational competencies is very likely to be similar. The specifics will differ to some degree. You'll find that many of the personal capability soft skill competencies are foundational to any industry or job function and expected to be exemplary if you are in a leadership role.

Assess Your Level of Competency

Begin with a self-assessment on the domains and capabilities in the Talent Development Capability Model or the model for your particular profession. There are job aids available on the ATD website (TD.org) that provide a deeper overview of the components of the model and how to access self-assessment tools. For other disciplines, professional associations similar to ATD will provide relevant information and resources.

Identify a Starting Point and Take Action

Your next step will be to identify a starting point to further develop your competency in the capabilities. The job aids and resources associated with the assessment should provide some guidance for how to determine your strengths and opportunities, and suggestions for development.

In general, you can follow steps similar to those outlined for engaging the influence principles as shown.

Based on the results of your self-assessment, identify areas where you're already doing well. What specific practices from these capabilities should you continue? Focus on being intentional about your actions on these areas of strength first. These will benefit you the most.

Which areas may need more attention for further development? Ask yourself the following questions:

- Given your current role, the current work environment you're in, or present situation, which competency do you believe would be most beneficial to focus on first? Select one competency as a starting point.
- What stood out to you when you reflected on why you gave yourself this rating?
- What steps should you take to meet the level of expectations for this competency?
  - What one step can you take in the next seven days that will benefit you most?

Challenge yourself to not be complacent and commit yourself to becoming a respected person of influence. Follow a development process of self-awareness, taking action, reviewing your progress, and making adjustments. Remember this is a journey, not a sprint.

Jimmy Nelson shared with me how, in his experience, personal accountability is typically already part of a talent development professional's DNA: "Maybe it's a level of internal personal accountability that you need to have as a learning and development professional, even beyond other professionals, where that inside internal accountability is what guides you. It's where I want to be."

Growing Influence With SCALE Competency Across Your Organization

As employees interact day-to-day to get things done, the ability to move others toward a common objective is essential. How influence works in your organization is reflective of how individuals and working relationships are valued and honored. Investing in the growth of people of influence across your organization produces a valuable return. Social capital produces a work environment where people are connected to their jobs and their colleagues in inclusive and authentic ways. Their depth of technical expertise and institutional knowledge enable them to courageously challenge the status quo, contributing with passion to the organization's bottom line and reputation. They both embody and create your organization's values.

One of the first steps you can take toward developing influence competency across your organization is to reinforce your organization's values. Provide clarity around the expectations for how values play a role in employee interactions, in fostering working relationships, and in how influence is cultivated. The core values of respect and integrity, for example, guide employees in how influence occurs and grows in a constructive and productive manner. In high-performing workplaces, influence is not manipulative or coercive.

The foundational influence with SCALE principles discussed in this book can also be taught to professionals at all levels within your organization. You can help others adopt these influence principles by modeling them and developing training programs to integrate these skills within the culture.

When you model the behaviors, make others aware of the principles you are modeling and why they are important. For example, people are often so busy, it's hard to find the time to invest in personal development. Identify a certificate program or skill that will enhance your knowledge and value. Schedule the training and study time on your calendar. Share with others how this will benefit you personally and the organization, and how you expect it may enhance your ability to be a greater influence through your role.

Develop an influence soft skills training program that, similar to personal development, focuses on building self-awareness of current practices and building competency in the influence with SCALE principles. Your organization should already have outlined core values and behavioral expectations for leaders and individual contributors. Influence should be elevated as a priority among those identified competencies.

Recognize how individuals are growing in and embodying these influence principles. Where are you seeing the impact on individual, team, and organizational performance?

Scale Your Influence

Now is an exciting time for talent development. With the speed of vast change we are experiencing, talent development is in a unique position to have a tremendous influence on the organizational capacity to keep up with and lead change.

Are you ready to step into that role? Are you ready to be that person of influence you have the potential to be?

Acknowledgments

Meet the Leaders Interviewed for This Book

To prepare for this book, I held a series of interviews and discussions with prominent business leaders. I am most appreciative for their generosity in sharing their experiences, perspectives, lessons learned, and best practices.

Sandi Maxey, MBA

Sandi Maxey is the vice president and director of talent development for Sandy Spring Bank, which she joined in 1999. She has been in banking for over 30 years with more than 25 years in learning and development. Her areas of expertise include leadership development, coaching, career development, and succession planning. Sandi is a graduate of the ABA Stonier Graduate School of Banking and a contributor to the ATD Press book *Leading the Learning Function*. Her professional credentials include MBTI and EQI 2.0 qualified, Crucial Conversations certified, CCL certified feedback facilitator, and a Bridges certified trainer.

Jimmy A. Nelson, PhD, CPTD, SHRM-SCP

Jimmy A. Nelson has served as both an organizational leader and consultant in the learning and organization development field for more than 30 years. He holds a master's in organizational development and training and a PhD in industrial organizational psychology; in addition, he has been an adjunct instructor at several universities. He is the author of the book, *Eat Your Green Peppers*. He taught the Dale Carnegie course for five years, and is certified in a multitude of assessments (including

Myers-Briggs, DiSC, Hogan, DDI, and PI.). His certifications include 7 Habits Certified Instructor, Certified Professional in Talent Development (CPTD) and the SHRM-SCP (Senior Certified Professional). Jimmy's current role is the director of organizational development and training with a multinational organization. Jimmy also serves on two nonprofit boards (VOA and Life Adventures Center), and is the past-president and frequent contributor to the ATD Kentuckiana Chapter (in addition to three years as a National Advisors for Chapter, Mid South Region). Jimmy's mission in life is "to completely exhaust my God given talents, before I die."

Amy K. Shilliday, CPTD

Amy K. Shilliday has extensive experience in training and development for customer support and B-to-B organizations. These experiences include senior trainer roles with mortgage banking, a top-three global media company, and one of the largest internet travel companies. Amy has spent serious time working on creating diverse learning delivery methods and design implementations that successfully develop organizations' service and sales teams. From adult learning theory to training the trainer to public speaking, Amy's skills have made her the amazing learning and development professional she is today. Amy is a frequent Association for Talent Development contributor and has served on ATD's International Conference & Exposition Program Advisory Committee. A passionate advocate for others in the TD industry, Amy occasionally volunteers for projects that support the ATD Certification Institute.

APPENDIX

Resources

Use these job aids, tools, and resources in the following pages to help you begin an accelerated transformation toward becoming a person of influence. Resources are also available for download at InfluenceWithScale.com.

My Personal Value Inventory

Our influence grows as we build social capital by selflessly adding value in our working relationships. Sometimes we feel like we have little to contribute in value to others. You have more to contribute than you may realize.

Considering the following categories, take a personal inventory of the assets you possess. Each of these areas offers potential for contributing value across your professional circle.

My special skills, abilities, and expertise:

_____

_____

My domain knowledge and experience:

_____

_____

My certificates, certifications, and professional accreditations:

_____

_____

Access to resources:

_____

_____

My network and contacts:

_____

_____

Career and professional experiences:

_____

_____

In what ways might I be able to use these assets to add value in my working relationships with my colleagues, my team, customers, and in my organization?

_____

_____

Embrace the Challenge:
Assess What You're Dealing With Decision Tool

When faced with a difficult or uncomfortable situation, assessing the realities more carefully can help you determine if and how you might proceed. Making an informed decision can boost your courage and influence. This list of questions can serve as a tool in embracing the challenge and making a thoughtful decision on how to move ahead.

Describe the challenge:

_____

_____

What are the facts?

_____

_____

How important is this concern to address? (0 = Not at all important; 5 = Very important)

_____

_____

What is the worst possible outcome?

_____

_____

What is the best possible result for all involved?

_____

_____

What options do I have for addressing this challenge?

_____

_____

What are the pros and cons of each option?

_____

_____

What steps can I take to realize the best possible result?

_____

_____

How might my personal and our organizational values influence my decisions and actions?

_____

_____

Practice Vulnerability Resources

Books and Related Content
Brown, Brene. *Dare to Lead.* Random House. 2018. (Book and workbook)
https://daretolead.brenebrown.com

Dare to Lead Podcast: https://brenebrown.com/dtl-podcast/

Assessment Tools

This table presents several of the behavior and personality assessments I am most familiar with and can recommend. This is by no means an exhaustive list of assessment tools on the market.

Source	Assessments	Where to Locate
TTI Success Insights	• Behaviors (DiSC) • Driving Forces • Soft Skills • Emotional Intelligence • 360-degree Feedback • Stress	ttisi.com
SHL	• SHL Occupational Personality Questionnaire (OPQ) • SHL Motivation Questionnaire (MQ) • Universal Competency Framework (UCF)	shl.com
The Myers-Briggs Company	• Myers-Briggs Type Indicator (MBTI)	mbtionline.com
Hogan Assessments	• Hogan Personality Inventory • Hogan Development Survey • Motives, Values, Preferences Inventory	hoganassessments.com
The Predictive Index	• The Predictive Index Behavioral Assessment	predictiveindex.com

Tap Into "Why" Resources

Assessments

Source	Assessments	Where to Locate
TTI Success Insights	Driving Forces	https://www.ttisi.com
SHL	SHL Motivation Questionnaire (MQ)	https://www.shl.com
Hogan Assessments	Motives, Values, Preferences Inventory	https://www.hoganassessments.com
The Predictive Index	The Predictive Index Behavioral Assessment	https://www.predictiveindex.com

Books and Related Content

Start With Why: How Great Leaders Inspire Everyone to Take Action https://simonsinek.com/product/start-with-why/

Simon Sinek's Ted Talk, "How Great Leaders Inspire Action" https://www.ted.com/talks/simon_sinek_how_great_leaders_inspire_action?language=en#t-1137092

Diversity and Inclusion Resources

Diversity Wheel
Primary & Secondary Dimensions of Diversity
Marilyn Loden | Loden Associates, Inc.
www.loden.com/Web_Stuff/Dimensions.html

Table of Diversity
Intersectional Dimensions of Diversity
Demetria Miles-McDonald | Decide Diversity
www.tableofdiversity.com

Inspire Belonging and Engagement:
Exploring My Own Dimensions of Diversity Discovery Tool

To inspire belonging and engagement within your team and organization, begin with exploring the dimensions of diversity you identify with yourself. Refer to the Diversity Wheel and/or Table of Diversity tool as you reflect on the following questions.

A. Identify the top five diversity dimensions that relate the most to how you see yourself.

1. _____

2. _____

3. _____

4. _____

5. _____

Why these five?

_____

_____

What privileges have these dimensions afforded you in your life?

_____

_____

What barriers have been present for you as a result of these dimensions of your identity?

_____

_____

How has that impacted your self-perception? How others see you?

_____

_____

What related life experiences stand out for you?

_____

_____

B. Identify the diversity dimensions that least represent you.

1. _____

2. _____

3. _____

4. _____

5. _____

What groups are representative of the dimensions you are least familiar or comfortable with? These can be a starting point for where you make intentional connections with others.

_____

_____

Assess Your Competency Across the Influence With SCALE Principles

Given what you have learned about each of the Influence With SCALE principles in this book, how would you rate your current practice in each?

- Circle your rating and answer the reflection questions for each principle.
- After completing your ratings and reflections, record your ratings for each of the five principles in Table 10-1 in chapter 10.
- Follow the steps outlined after the table to identify a starting point and take action.

How would I rate my current practice?

Social Capital   1   2   3   4   5

What is the reason for your rating?

_____

_____

Are there certain practices or situations that come to mind?

_____

_____

Courage   1   2   3   4   5

What is the reason for your rating?

_____

_____

Are there certain practices or situations that come to mind?

_____

_____

Authenticity   1   2   3   4   5
What is the reason for your rating?

_____

_____

Are there certain practices or situations that come to mind?

_____

_____

Leaning in With Passion   1   2   3   4   5
What is the reason for your rating?

_____

_____

Are there certain practices or situations that come to mind?

_____

_____

Engaging a Diverse and Inclusive Workplace Community   1   2   3   4   5
What is the reason for your rating?

_____

_____

Are there certain practices or situations that come to mind?

_____

_____

References

Abrams, A. 2018. "Yes, Impostor Syndrome Is Real. Here's How to Deal With It." *Time*, June 20. time.com/5312483/how-to-deal-with-impostor-syndrome.

American Psychological Association (APA). 2020. "Persuasion." APA Dictionary of Psychology. dictionary.apa.org/persuasion.

Aquino, A., F.R. Alparone, S. Pagliaro, et al. 2020. "Sense or Sensibility? The Neuro-Functional Basis of the Structural Matching Effect in Persuasion." *Cognitive Affect Behavioral Neuroscience* 20:536–550.

Association for Talent Development (ATD). 2019. "The Talent Development Capability Model." TD.org. d22bbllmj4tvv8.cloudfront.net/18/5b/1142b292431fb5393f2193211e1b/talent-development-capability-model-definitions.pdf.

Association for Talent Development (ATD). 2018. *Bridging the Skills Gap: Workforce Development and the Future of Work*. Alexandria, VA: ATD Press.

Baggs, R.K. 2019. "Being an Influencer and Being Influential Are Not the Same Thing." Fstoppers, October 12. fstoppers.com/originals/being-influencer-and-being-influential-are-not-same-thing-416462.

Bersin, J. 2017. *Future of Work: The People Imperative*. Deloitte, October.

BetterUp Labs. 2019. The Value of Belonging at Work: New Frontiers for Inclusion. BetterUp. get.betterup.co/rs/600-WTC-654/images/BetterUp_BelongingReport_091019.pdf.

Bingham, T. 2014. "Talent Development." ATD Insights, May 21. td.org/insights/talent-development.

Biographyonline.net. 2017. "100 Most Influential People in the World." Biography Online. biographyonline.net/people/100-most -influential.html.

Blaschka, A. 2019. "The Number One Soft Skill Employers Seek." *Forbes*. forbes.com/sites/amyblaschka/2019/02/28/the-number-one-soft-skill-employers-seek-and-five-ways-top-leaders-say-to-cultivate-yours.

Bonnstetter, B.J., and J.l. Suiter. 2018. *The Universal Language DISC Reference Manual*. TTI Success Insights.

Buote, V. 2016. "Most Employees Feel Authentic at Work, But It Can Take a While." *Harvard Business Review*, May 11. hbr.org/2016/05/mos t-employees-feel-authentic-at-work-but-it-can-take-a-while.

Burton, N. 2019. "The Art of Persuasion." *Psychology Today*, June 16. psychologytoday.com/us/blog/hide-and-seek/201906/the-art-persuasion.

Business Insider. 2021. "Influencer Marketing: Social Media Influence Market Stats and Research for 2021." *Business Insider*, January 6. businessinsider.com/influencer-marketing-report.

Cameron, K., C. Mora, T. Leutscher, and M. Calarco. 2011. "Effects of Positive Practices on Organizational Effectiveness." *Journal of Applied Behavioral Science* 47(3): 266–308.

Carr, E.W., A. Reece, G. Rosen Kellerman, and A. Robichaux. 2019. "The Value of Belonging at Work." *Harvard Business Review*, December 16. hbr.org/2019/12/the-value-of-belonging-at-work.

Chadsey, J., and S. Beyer. 2001. "Social Relationships in the Workplace." *Mental Retardation and Developmental Disabilities Research Reviews* 7(2): 128–133.

Chandler, M., et al. 2019. "LinkedIn Global Talent Trends." LinkedIn Talent Solutions. business.linkedin.com/content/dam/me/business/ en-us/talent-solutions/resources/pdfs/global-talent-trends-2019.pdf.

Cialdini, R. 1984. *Influence: The Psychology of Persuasion*. New York: HarperCollins Books.

Cialdini, R. 2016a. "The Principles of Persuasion Aren't Just for Business." *Influence at Work*, May 23.

Cialdini, R. 2016b. *Pre-Suasion: A Revolutionary Way to Influence and Persuade*. New York: Simon and Schuster.

Cialdini, R., and S. Cliffe. 2013. "The Uses (and Abuses) of Influence." *Harvard Business Review*, July-August.

Clayton, M. 2018. *Imposter Syndrome*. London: Management Pocketbooks.

Coutu, D. 2007. "Making Relationships Work." *Harvard Business Review*, December.

Covey, S.R. 1989. *The Seven Habits of Highly Effective People*. New York: Simon & Schuster.

Dalla-Camina, M. 2018. "The Reality of Imposter Syndrome." *Psychology Today*, September 3. psychologytoday.com/us/blog/real-women/201809/the-reality-imposter-syndrome.

Davis, J. 2019. *The Art of Quiet Influence: Timeless Wisdom for Leading Without Authority*. Boston: Nicholas Brealey.

DeFalco, N. 2009. "Influence vs. Persuasion: A Critical Distinction for Leaders." *Social Media Today*, October 30.

DeakinCo. 2017. "Soft Skills for Business Success." Deloitte Access Economics. deakinco.com/uploads/Whitepaper/deloitte-au-economics-deakin-soft-skills-business-success-170517.pdf.

Deloitte. 2013. *Waiter, Is That Inclusion in My Soup? A New Recipe to Improve Business Performance*. Deloitte. deloitte.com/content/dam/Deloitte/au/Documents/human-capital/deloitte-au-hc-diversity-inclusion-soup-0513.pdf.

Deloitte. 2019. *Leading the Social Enterprise: Reinvent with a Human Focus*. Deloitte Global Human Capital Trends. deloitte.com/content/dam/insights/us/articles/5136_HC-Trends-2019/DI_HC-Trends-2019.pdf.

Demarest, P. 2020. "Neuro-Axiology Part One: Foundational Principles and Practices of a Game-Changing Model for High-Value Coaching." WBECS Full Summit Session, October 15.

DeMers, J. 2015. "7 Ways to Build Influence in the Workplace." Inc.com, January 15. inc.com/jayson-demers/7-ways-to-build-influence-in-the-workplace.html.

Derven, M. 2015. "D&I and Talent Management: Made for Each Other." ATD Insights, April 7. td.org/insights/d-i-and-talent-management-made-for-each-other.

Detert, J.R. 2018. "Cultivating Everyday Courage." *Harvard Business Review*, November–December. hbr.org/2018/11/cultivating-everyday-courage.

Dictionary.com. n.d. "Respect Definitions." dictionary.com/browse/respect.

Discenza, R., and J.B. Forman. 2007. "Seven Causes of Project Failure: How to Recognize Them and How to Initiate Project Recovery." Paper presented at PMI Global Congress 2007—North America, Atlanta, GA. Newtown Square, PA: Project Management Institute.

Dixon-Fyle, S., V. Hunt, K. Dolan, and S. Prince. 2020. *Diversity Wins: How Inclusion Matters*. McKinsey & Company, May.

Duarte, N. 2015. "To Win People Over, Speak to Their Wants and Needs." *Harvard Business Review*, May 12. hbr.org/2015/05/to-win-people-over-speak-to-their-wants-and-needs.

Elliott, C. 2015. "Coaching Leaders With Influence vs. Power." *About Leaders*, October 22. aboutleaders.com/coaching-leaders-with-influence-vs-power/#gs.1q0faa.

Ellis, R.K. 2018. "Revolution 4.0." *TD*, November.

Enns, H.G., and D.B. McFarlin. 2005. "When Executives Successfully Influence Peers: The Role of Target Assessment, Preparation, and Tactics." *Human Resource Management*, August 23.

Fairholm, G.W. 1998. *Perspectives on Leadership: From the Science of Management to Its Spiritual Heart*. Santa Barbara, CA: Praeger.

Fazal, A. 2020. "The Importance of D&I in the Workplace." *HR Daily Advisor*, April 16. hrdailyadvisor.blr.com/2020/04/16/the-importance-of-di-in-the-workplace.

Fellizar, K. 2019. "7 Signs Someone May Have a Superiority Complex." *Bustle*, April 3. bustle.com/p/7-signs-someone-may-have-a -superiority-complex-17006240.

Feser, C. 2016. *When Execution Isn't Enough: Decoding Inspirational Leadership.* Hoboken, NJ: John Wiley & Sons.

Finfgeld, D.L. 1999. "Courage as a Process of Pushing Beyond the Struggle." *Qualitative Health Research*, November.

Gallup. 2016. *The Relationship Between Engagement at Work and Organizational Outcomes, 2016 Q12® Meta-Analysis: Ninth Edition.* news. gallup.com/reports/191489/q12-meta-analysis-report-2016.aspx.

Gallup. 2017. *State of the American Workplace.* gallup.com/workplace/ 238085/state-american-workplace-report-2017.aspx.

Ganjehsani, W. 2019. "How Human Performance Improvement Can Transform Businesses." ATD Insights, April 29. td.org/user/content/ wandaganjehsani/how-human-performance-improvement-can -transform-businesses-03-29-19-07-52.

Gautrey, C. 2017. "The Ethics of Influence: Five Rules to Live By." *Learn to Influence*, August 8. learntoinfluence.com/the-ethics-of-influence -five-rules-to-live-by.

Geggel, L. 2015. "Chameleons' Color-Changing Secret Revealed." LiveScience.com, March 10. livescience.com/50096-chameleons -color-change.html.

Geue, P.E. 2018. "Positive Practices in the Workplace: Impact on Team Climate, Work Engagement, and Task Performance." *Journal of Applied Behavioral Science* 10(1): 70–99.

Gholston, S. 2020. "A Closer Look at In-Demand Soft Skills." *TD*, June. td.org/magazines/td-magazine/a-closer-look-at-in-demand-soft-skills.

Glassdoor. 2020. "Best Places to Work 2020 Employee's Choice." glassdoor. com/Award/Best-Places-to-Work-LST_KQ0,19.htm.

Godin, S. 2017. "Let's Stop Calling Them 'Soft Skills.'" It's Your Turn Blog, January. itsyourturnblog.com/lets-stop-calling-them-soft-skills-9cc27ec09ecb.

Godin, S. 2008. *Tribes*. New York: Penguin.

Goleman, D. 2013. *Primal Leadership: Unleashing the Power of Emotional Intelligence*. Boston: Harvard Business School Publishing.

Grier, S. 2012. "How Passion For Your Job Can Lead To Success." *IT Managers Inbox*. itmanagersinbox.com/1559/how-passion-for-your-job-can-lead-to-success.

Gurchiek, K. 2018. "6 Steps for Building an Inclusive Workplace." *HR Daily Advisor*, March 19. shrm.org/hr-today/news/hr-magazine/0418/pages/6-steps-for-building-an-inclusive-workplace.aspx.

Hagel, J., J. Seely Brown, A. Ranjan, and D. Byler. 2014. *Passion at Work: Cultivating Worker Passion as a Cornerstone of Talent Development*. Deloitte.

Hallak, D. 2014. "Five Networks to Accelerate Your Career." *TD*, October. td.org/magazines/td-magazine/five-networks-to-accelerate-your-career.

Halvorson, H. 2013. "What It Takes to Have Influence." *Psychology Today*, February 20. psychologytoday.com/us/blog/the-science-success/201302/what-it-takes-have-influence.

Hatch, M.J. 1993. "The Dynamics of Organizational Culture." *Academy of Management Review*, October.

Hill, L.A., and K. Lineback. 2015. "3 Things Managers Should Be Doing Every Day." *Harvard Business Review*, September 24.

History Collection. Nd. "40 of the Most Influential People of All Time." History Collection.com. historycollection.com/40-of-the-most-influential-people-of-all-time.

Holland, K. 2019. "What Is a Superiority Complex?" Healthline, August 29. healthline.com/health/mental-health/superiority-complex.

Horsager, D. 2011. *The Trust Edge*. Minneapolis, MN: Summerside Press.

Houston, E. Nd. "The Importance of Positive Relationships in the Workplace." positivepsychology.com. positivepsychology.com/positive-relationships-workplace.

Indeed Editorial Team. 2020. "Developing Personal Ethics: Examples and Tips." Indeed.com, September 7. indeed.com/career-advice/career-development/developing-personal-ethics.

Jackson, T. 2017. "Leadership Skills: Persuasion and Influence." *About Leaders*, May 16. aboutleaders.com/leadership-skills-persuasion-and-influence/#gs.wrydua.

Johnson, S.K. 2020. "How CEOs Can Lead Selflessly Through a Crisis." *Harvard Business Review*, May 14. hbr.org/2020/05/how-ceos-can-lead-selflessly-through-a-crisis.

Jones J.R., D.C. Wilson, and P. Jones. 2008. "Toward Achieving the 'Beloved Community' in the Workplace: Lessons for Applied Business Research and Practice From the Teachings of Martin Luther King Jr." *Business & Society* 47(4): 457–483.

Kambouris, A. 2018. "The 7 Leadership Building Blocks for Courageous Workplaces." Entrepreneurer.com, May 30. entrepreneur.com/article/313505.

Kamdar, D., and L. Van Dyne. 2007. "The Joint Effects of Personality and Workplace Social Exchange Relationships in Predicting Task Performance and Citizenship Performance." *Journal of Applied Psychology* 92(5): 1286–1298.

Kets de Vries, M.F.R. 2020. "How to Find and Practice Courage." *Harvard Business Review*, May 12. hbr.org/2020/05/how-to-find-and-practice-courage.

Kipnis, D., S.M. Schmidt, and I. Wilkinson. 1980. "Intraorganizational Influence Tactics: Explorations in Getting One's Way." *Journal of Applied Psychology* 65(4): 440–452.

Klein, K.J., and T. D'Aunno. 1986. "Psychological Sense of Community in the Workplace." *Journal of Community Psychology* 14(4): 365–377.

Kouzes, J., and B. Posner. 1995. *The Leadership Challenge*. San Francisco: Jossey-Bass Publishers.

Lederman, M.T. 2012. *The 11 Laws of Likability*. New York: American Management Association.

Leonard, K. 2019. "Importance of Workplace Diversity." *Chron*, March 16. smallbusiness.chron.com/importance-workplace-diversity-43235.

LinkedIn. 2020. "2020 Workplace Learning Report." LinkedIn. learning. linkedin.com/content/dam/me/learning/resources/pdfs/ LinkedIn-Learning-2020-Workplace-Learning-Report.pdf.

Loden, M. n.d. "Primary & Secondary Dimensions of Diversity." Loden. com. loden.com/Web_Stuff/Dimensions.

Lomenick, B. 2018. "6 Steps Toward a Courageous Organization." *Outreach Magazine*, January 18. outreachmagazine.com/features/10870-6-steps-toward-a-courageous-organization.html.

Lustberg, A. 2008. *How to Sell Yourself: Using Leadership, Likability and Luck to Succeed*. Career Press.

Luttrell, A. 2020. "Why Persuasion Is Personal: The Neuroscience of Influence." *Psychology Today*, June 20.

Mackey, Z. 2018. "Diversity AND Inclusion in The Workplace Equals Equality." BK Connection, June 15. ideas.bkconnection.com/why-diversity-is-not-enough-inclusion-equals-equality.

Manion, J., and K. Bartholomew. 2004. "Community in the Workplace: A Proven Retention Strategy." *Journal of Nursing Administration* 34(1): 46–53.

Manville, B. 2016. "Building Community as if People Mattered." *Forbes*, November 6. forbes.com/sites/brookmanville/2016/11/06/building-community-as-if-people-mattered.

Mascetta, P. 2012. *The Code of Influence*. Self-published.

Maxey, S. 2021. Conversation with the author.

McMillan, D.W., and D.M. Chavis. 1986. "Sense of Community: A Definition and Theory." *Journal of Community Psychology* 4(1): 6–23.

Merriam-Webster. n.d. "Courage definition." *Merriam-Webster's Dictionary*. merriam-webster.com.

Miles-McDonald, D. n.d. "Table of Diversity." Decided Diversity. decidediversity.com/tableofdiversity.

Mintzberg, H. 2009. "Rebuilding Companies as Communities." *Harvard Business Review*, July-August.

Mintzberg, H. 2018. "Communityship Beyond Leadership." Mintzberg Blog, November 18. mintzberg.org/blog/communityship-beyond -leadership.

Monahan, K. 2016. "Why Relationships Matter at Work." LinkedIn, October 10. linkedin.com/pulse/why-relationships-matter-work -kelly-monahan-ph-d.

Moran, G. 2019. "Building Influence in the Workplace." *Fast Company*, June 18. fastcompany.com/90364946/building-influence-in-the -workplace.

Morgan, N. 2015. "Understand the 4 Components of Influence." *Harvard Business Review*, May 19. hbr.org/2015/05/understand -the-4-components-of-influence.

Muller, A., L. Sirianni, and R. Addante. 2019. "Neural Correlates of the Dunning-Kruger Effect." *European Journal of Neuroscience*, December 24.

Musselwhite, C., and T. Plouffe. 2012. "What's Your Influencing Style?" *Harvard Business Review*, January 13. hbr.org/2012/01/whats-your -influencing-style.

Nahai, N., and R. Dreeke. 2013. "Trust, Persuasion and Manipulation." *Psychology Today*, September 21. psychologytoday.com/us/blog/webs -influence/201309/trust-persuasion-and-manipulation.

Nance-Nash, S., and B.D. Norton. 2020. "Why Imposter Syndrome Hits Women and Women of Colour Harder." BBC, July 27. bbc.com/ worklife/article/20190722-welcome-to-bbc-worklife.

Naylor, T.H., W.H. Willimon, and R. Oesterberg. 1996. "The Search for Community in the Workplace." *Business & Society Review* 97(97): 42–47.

Naylor, T.H., W.H. Willimon, and R.V. Osterberg. 2002. *The Search for Meaning in the Workplace*. San Francisco: Berrett-Koehler.

Nelson, J. 2021. Conversation with the author.

O'Hara, C. 2014. "Proven Ways to Earn Your Employees' Trust." *Harvard Business Review*, June 27.

Papini, J. 2020. "Key Components for Cultivating Inclusion." ATD Insights, February 14. td.org/insights/keys-component-for-cultivating-inclusion.

Parsi, N. 2017. "Workplace Diversity and Inclusion Gets Innovative." *HR Magazine*, January 16. shrm.org/hr-today/news/hr-magazine/0217/pages/disrupting-diversity-in-the-workplace.aspx.

Pavlovich, L. n.d. *Research Review of Personality and Behavioral Assessments*. Athletic Assessments. athleteassessments.com/personality-and-behavioral-assessments.

Perme, C. 2016a. "Organizational Courage: How to Build It." Human Synergistics International, May 4. humansynergistics.com/blog/constructive-culture-blog/details/constructive-culture/2016/05/04/organizational-courage-part-2-of-2-how-to-build-it.

Perme, C. 2016b. "Organizational Courage: What It Is." Human Synergistics International, April 11. humansynergistics.com/blog/constructive-culture-blog/details/constructive-culture/2016/04/11/organizational-courage-part-1-of-2-what-it-is.

Pink, D.H. 2021. *To Sell is Human: The Surprising Truth About Moving Others*. San Francisco: Riverhead Books.

Psychology Today. n.d.a. "Ethics and Morality." *Psychology Today*. psychologytoday.com/us/basics/ethics-and-morality.

Psychology Today. n.d.b. "Big 5 Personality Traits." *Psychology Today*. psychologytoday.com/us/basics/big-5-personality-traits.

Psychology Today. n.d.c. "Imposter Syndrome." *Psychology Today*. psychologytoday.com/us/basics/imposter-syndrome.

Reardon, K.K. 2007. "Courage as a Skill." *Harvard Business Review*, January. hbr.org/2007/01/courage-as-a-skill.

Regier, N. 2019. "Move From Diversity to Inclusion With the Compassion Mindset," ATD Insights, July 25. td.org/insights/move-from-diversity -to-inclusion-with-the-compassion-mindset.

Reina, D., and M. Reina. 2010. *Rebuilding Trust in the Workplace: Seven Steps to Renew Confidence, Commitment, and Energy.* Alexandria, VA: ASTD Press.

Rogers, K. 2018. "Do Your Employees Feel Respected?" *Harvard Business Review*, July-August. hbr.org/2018/07/do-your-employees-feel -respected.

Roosevelt, T. n.d. "People Don't Care How Much You Know Until They Know How Much You Care." Goodreads Quotes. goodreads.com/ quotes/34690-people-don-t-care-how-much-you-know-until-they -know.

Rosh, L., and L. Offermann. 2013. "Be Yourself, but Carefully." *Harvard Business Review*, October. hbr.org/2013/10/be-yourself-but-carefully.

Rowell, D. 2019. "3 Traits of a Strong Professional Relationship." *Harvard Business Review*, August 8. hbr.org/2019/08/3-traits-of-a-strong -professional-relationship.

Sakulku, J., and J. Alexander. 2011. "The Impostor Phenomenon." *International Journal of Behavioral Science* 6(1): 75–97.

Sanghera, P. 2019. CAPM in Depth. Boston: Cengage.

Sanjeev, M.A., and A.V. Surya. 2016. "Two Factor Theory of Motivation and Satisfaction: An Empirical Verification." *Annals of Data Science* 3:155–173.

Seiter, C. 2015. "How Changing One Word in Job Descriptions Can Lead To More Diverse Can Lead to More Diverse Candidates." *Fast Company*, March 24. fastcompany.com/3044094/how-changing-one -word-in-job-descriptions-can-lead-to-more-diverse-candid.

Shaffer, C.R., and K. Anundsen. 1993. *Creating Community Anywhere: Finding Support and Connection in a Fragmented World*. New York: Penguin.

Shilliday, A. 2021. Conversation with the author.

Sias, P.M. 2009. *Organizing Relationships | Traditional and Emerging Perspectives on Workplace Relationships*. Los Angeles: SAGE Publications.

Sinek, S. 2009. "How Great Leaders Inspire Action." TEDxPuget Sound, video. ted.com/talks/simon_sinek_how_great_leaders_inspire_action?language=en#t-1137092.

Society for Human Resource Management (SHRM). 2016. *The New Talent Landscape: Recruiting Difficulty and Skills Shortages*. Alexandria, VA: SHRM.

Society for Human Resource Management (SHRM). 2019. *The Global Skills Shortage: Bridging the Talent Gap with Education, Training and Sourcing*. Alexandria, VA: SHRM.

Southgate, J. 2018. "3 Methods to Influence SMEs." *TD* magazine, April. td.org/magazines/td-magazine/3-methods-to-influence-smes.

Spehar, I., J. Forest, and F. Stenseng. 2016. "Passion for Work, Job Satisfaction, and the Mediating Role of Belongingness." *Scandinavian Journal of Organizational Psychology*, May.

Spinks, D. 2016. "The 10-Step Process for Building a Thriving Community from Scratch." CMX. cmxhub.com/build-a-thriving-community-from-scratch.

TTI Success Insights. 2017. *12 Driving Forces Manual® Reference Guide*. TTI Success Insights. ttisi.com.

TTI Success Insights. 2018. *Emotional Quotient (EQ) Manual*. TTI Success Insights. ttisi.com.

Van den Bosch, R., and T.W. Taris. 2014. "Authenticity at Work: Development and Validation of an Individual Authenticity Measure at Work." *Journal of Happiness Studies*, February.

Van den Bosch, R., T.W. Taris, W.B. Schaufeli, M.C.W. Peeters, and G. Reijseger. 2019. "Authenticity at Work: A Matter of Fit?" *The Journal of Psychology* 153(2): 247–266.

van Gogh, V. 1881. "Letter to Theo van Gogh." Written December 29, 1881, in The Hague. Translated by Johanna van Gogh-Bonger. Edited by Robert Harrison. No. 166.

van Knippenbe, B., D. van Knippenbe, E. Blaau, and R. Vermunt. 1999. "Relational Considerations in the Use of Influence Tactics." *Journal of Applied Social Psychology* 29(4): 806–819.

Vezich, I.S., P.L. Katzman, D.L. Ames, E.B. Falk, and M.D. Lieberman. 2017. "Modulating the Neural Bases of Persuasion: Why/How, Gain/Loss, and Users/Non-Users." *Social Cognitive and Affective Neuroscience* 12(2): 283–297.

Warrell, M. 2021. "Build A Culture That Fuels Courage, Not Fear." *Forbes*, February 7. forbes.com/sites/margiewarrell/2021/02/07/build-a -culture-that-fuels-courage-not-fear.

Whiting, K. 2020. "Top Ten Skills of 2025: The 4 Trends Transforming Your Workplace." World Economic Forum, October. weforum.org/ agenda/2020/10/top-10-work-skills-of-tomorrow-how-long-it-takes -to-learn-them.

Williamson, T. 2018. "How to Build a Culture of Bold and Courageous Leaders." *Forbes*, April 30. forbes.com/sites/forbescoachescouncil/ 2018/04/30/how-to-build-a-culture-of-bold-and-courageous -leaders.

Zemke, R. 1996. "The Call of Community." *Training* 33(March): 27.

Zhu, P. 2017. "Likability vs. Respect vs. Trust." *Future of CIO*, January. futureofcio.blogspot.com/2017/01/likeability-vs-respect-vs-trust.html.

Index

Page numbers followed by *f* refer to figures.

trust
    building, xiv–xv, 32, 38
    foundation of, 9
    mutual, 41–43
    The Trust Edge (Horsager), 42
    TTI Success Insights, 80–81

V

value, 4, 39, 120–121
Van den Bosch, R., 76–77
Van Dyne, Linn, 45–46
van Gogh, Vincent, 55
ventromedial prefrontal cortex (vMPFC),
    16
virtual teams, 30
vulnerability, 60–61, 67–68, 122–123

W

Warrell, Margie, 61
When Execution Isn't Enough (Feser), 13–14
Williamson, Tameka, 55
Willimon, W.H., 119, 122
workplace community. *See* communities
World Economic Forum, viii

X

X-Y motivation theory, 50

Y

YouTube, 21

About the Author

Vivian Hairston Blade, MBA, MBB, PMP, is a recognized leadership expert and thought leader. As the President and CEO of Experts in Growth Leadership Consulting, she works with the world's top brands, equipping leaders with the resilience that inspires teams to recover quickly in the face of ongoing disruption and thrive in spite of insurmountable odds. Her impact is felt as a frequent speaker for association conferences, and in delivering transformative leadership development programs, executive coaching, and consulting for corporations.

Following a successful 20-year corporate career with Fortune 100 companies Humana and GE, Vivian launched her current leadership consulting practice, applying her extensive business, finance, and leadership experience to coach and develop aspiring and established leaders in building high-performance, high-quality, and high-service level organizations. She also works as adjunct faculty for the University of Louisville College of Business.

In addition to *Influence in Talent Development*, Vivian is the author of two books, *FuelForward: Discover Proven Practices to Fuel Your Career Forward*, which reveals the unwritten rules to career success, and *Resilience Ready: The Leader's Guide to Thriving Through Unrelenting Crises*. She is a contributor to two books published by the Association for Talent Development: *Find Your Fit: A Practical Guide to Landing a Job You'll Love* and *Work the Problem: How Experts Tackle Workplace Challenges*.

Vivian has served on the ATD International Conference & Exposition Program Advisory Committee, has presented conference workshops, has content featured in ATD webcasts, and her articles are featured on TD.org. She is also a member of the ATD Kentuckiana Chapter.

If you would like to have a consultation to explore support and solutions to your specific individual or organizational challenges, contact her through email (vivian@vivianblade.com), by phone (502.419.2433), or on her website (vivianblade.com).

You can also connect with Vivian via LinkedIn (linkedin.com/in/vivianblade), Twitter (@VivianBlade), and YouTube (youtube.com/c/VivianBlade).